PEOPLE OF NEW ZEALAND

BY SAM MOORE

ALLEN&UNWIN
SYDNEY · MELBOURNE · AUCKLAND · LONDON

CONTENTS

INTRODUCTION

New Zealand is a unique place. It's a country of stunning beauty, limitless opportunities . . . and some very interesting characters!

On a daily basis we encounter an incredibly diverse array of people. There are friendly passers-by looking to share their thoughts on the weather, and workmates hoping to impress with outrageous tales from the weekend.

There are the party animals and the home-bodies, the classic Kiwi dads and the quintessential Kiwi mums. There's the mainstream, the fringe and the just plain 'out there'; the ones trying desperately to conform, and the ones trying just as hard to look as though they're *not* conforming.

This book celebrates each and every one of those weird, wacky and thoroughly loveable creatures!

CAR ENTHUSIAST SHAE

It's Friday night and most lads Shae's age are probably on their fifth or sixth beer, but not Shae. Shae's smashing back an enormous energy drink in preparation for the evening's automobile-centred activities.

He and his best mates are about to jump in the '88 Nissan Cefiro (his pride and joy) and begin the cruise up Colombo Street. Following close behind Shae will be Matty in the Rotary, Justin in the Trueno and Sean in the Skyline GTS-T. The first stop will be the South City Shopping Centre car park, where Shae hopes to rendezvous with Stacey in her Galant VR4. He's had a crush on her ever since he saw her drift her way through a roundabout on Blenheim Road. Good luck with Stacey, mate!

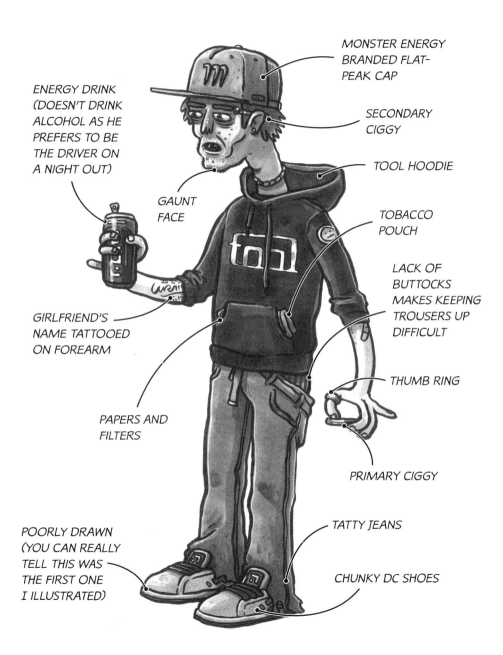

MONSTER ENERGY BRANDED FLAT-PEAK CAP

SECONDARY CIGGY

TOOL HOODIE

TOBACCO POUCH

LACK OF BUTTOCKS MAKES KEEPING TROUSERS UP DIFFICULT

THUMB RING

PRIMARY CIGGY

TATTY JEANS

CHUNKY DC SHOES

ENERGY DRINK (DOESN'T DRINK ALCOHOL AS HE PREFERS TO BE THE DRIVER ON A NIGHT OUT)

GAUNT FACE

GIRLFRIEND'S NAME TATTOOED ON FOREARM

PAPERS AND FILTERS

POORLY DRAWN (YOU CAN REALLY TELL THIS WAS THE FIRST ONE I ILLUSTRATED)

WORKSHOP TOM

Tom doesn't really look like the most approachable bloke, but underneath that rough, oil-stained exterior there's a gentle, unflinchingly helpful man. Tom's worked in the same engineering workshop for almost 50 years, he's a brilliantly methodical problem-solver, and there's nothing he can't fix. He sometimes gets frustrated with the quick-fix solutions of the younger employees, but Tom thinks back to when he first started out. They just need some experience, and he makes sure they learn from their mistakes. Any time Tom pops over for a cuppa, he'll be shaking door frames, straightening pictures and generally just checking everything around the house for strength and sturdiness. He's always there to offer a helping hand or give advice, even if you don't ask for it.

Hey, Tom, my mower blades are a bit blunt; reckon you could give me a hand sharpening 'em?

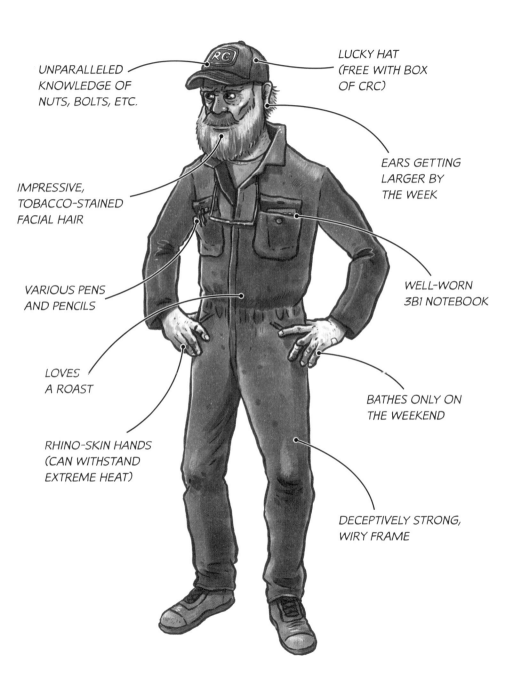

UNPARALLELED KNOWLEDGE OF NUTS, BOLTS, ETC.

LUCKY HAT (FREE WITH BOX OF CRC)

IMPRESSIVE, TOBACCO-STAINED FACIAL HAIR

EARS GETTING LARGER BY THE WEEK

VARIOUS PENS AND PENCILS

WELL-WORN 3B1 NOTEBOOK

LOVES A ROAST

BATHES ONLY ON THE WEEKEND

RHINO-SKIN HANDS (CAN WITHSTAND EXTREME HEAT)

DECEPTIVELY STRONG, WIRY FRAME

SALON OWNER TRISHA

Trisha started in the beauty industry when she was just 14 years old. During school holidays she'd work in her auntie's hair salon, sweeping floors, refilling spray bottles and just doing any odd job that needed doing. She loved everything about it: the gossip, the style and the smells. The best thing of all, though, was when the salon was quiet; she knew there was a chance the ladies would style her hair. She loved to see her mum's reaction when she would come home with a different cut or colour. She quickly moved up through the ranks, from floor sweeper to reception and then on to apprentice.

After almost a decade working for her auntie, Trisha knew she had to make a move and go out on her own. She'd been saving and planning for years, and she was confident in her ability. Today Trisha is the proud owner of her very own hair salon, with four fabulous employees and a long list of loyal clients. She hasn't forgotten her roots, though. The most rewarding part of her job is helping young people into the industry and seeing them develop into confident, skilled professionals. In the future, Trisha hopes to diversify her business by moving into nail art and eyelash extensions.

Good luck, Trisha!

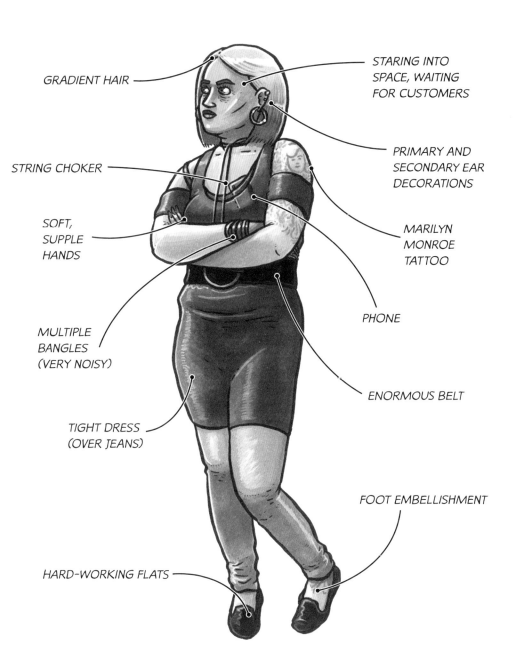

GRADIENT HAIR

STARING INTO SPACE, WAITING FOR CUSTOMERS

PRIMARY AND SECONDARY EAR DECORATIONS

STRING CHOKER

SOFT, SUPPLE HANDS

MARILYN MONROE TATTOO

PHONE

MULTIPLE BANGLES (VERY NOISY)

ENORMOUS BELT

TIGHT DRESS (OVER JEANS)

FOOT EMBELLISHMENT

HARD-WORKING FLATS

CAMPGROUND LEGEND MICKEY

Mickey is a legend 'round these parts; he's been coming to this same campground for almost all of his 55 years. He works hard for nine months of the year so he can enjoy three months of uninterrupted barbecues, naps, drink and fishing. Mickey knows almost everybody around here, and if he sees someone new, he'll be sure to introduce himself and show them around. Mickey books his holiday years in advance, so he always has the best spot, close to the beach and amenities. His super-honed camp set-up (the Palace) includes a three-room tent, food fridge, drinks fridge, TV (to watch the cricket), queen mattress and portable lighting. He's always up for a beer and a yarn, so if you see Mickey sitting back enjoying the good life, make sure you pop into the Palace and say hi.

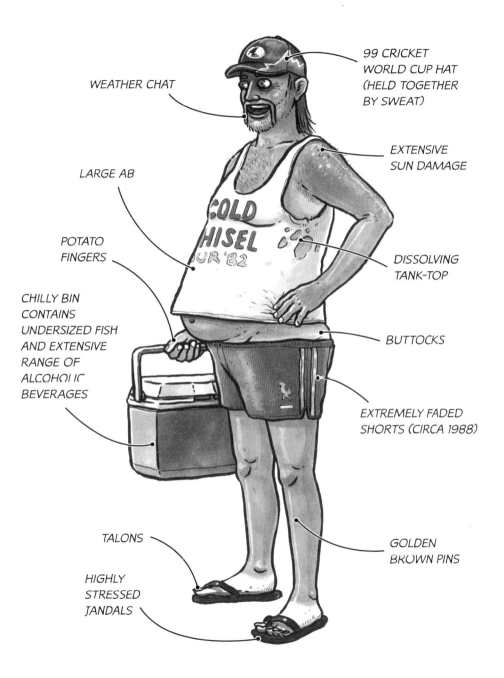

99 CRICKET WORLD CUP HAT (HELD TOGETHER BY SWEAT)

WEATHER CHAT

EXTENSIVE SUN DAMAGE

LARGE AB

POTATO FINGERS

DISSOLVING TANK-TOP

CHILLY BIN CONTAINS UNDERSIZED FISH AND EXTENSIVE RANGE OF ALCOHOLIC BEVERAGES

BUTTOCKS

EXTREMELY FADED SHORTS (CIRCA 1988)

TALONS

HIGHLY STRESSED JANDALS

GOLDEN BROWN PINS

ROAD WARRIOR CRAIG

During the week Craig likes to remain relatively anonymous, pushing paper at a medium-sized investment firm. But when Saturday morning hits, things change. Craig is a member of a local bicycle gang that terrorises local cafés and their hapless baristas. The 15-member clan has been known to clean out a café's milk supply in under 35 minutes. Socially, Craig has always struggled to find his place in the world, so joining the local chapter of the North Shore Road Warriors has been great for his confidence. He's finally found a way that he can express himself, whether it's through his inconsiderately tight Lycra or his high-tech, leg-powered crotch hog. At last, Craig feels comfortable in his own skin.

Ride on, Craig!

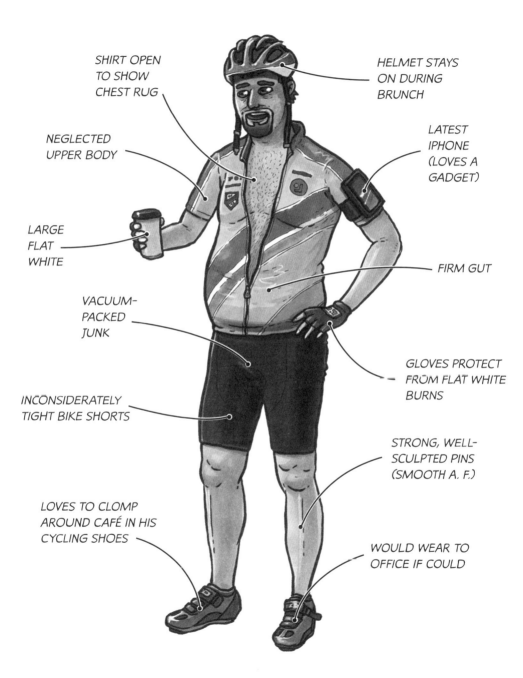

SHIRT OPEN TO SHOW CHEST RUG

HELMET STAYS ON DURING BRUNCH

NEGLECTED UPPER BODY

LATEST IPHONE (LOVES A GADGET)

LARGE FLAT WHITE

FIRM GUT

VACUUM-PACKED JUNK

GLOVES PROTECT FROM FLAT WHITE BURNS

INCONSIDERATELY TIGHT BIKE SHORTS

STRONG, WELL-SCULPTED PINS (SMOOTH A. F.)

LOVES TO CLOMP AROUND CAFÉ IN HIS CYCLING SHOES

WOULD WEAR TO OFFICE IF COULD

BEACH
DINNER
CAROL

Carol loves her three children to death, but she can't wait for the school holidays to end.

The past few months have been filled with road trips, movie nights, hot days in the back yard playing under the sprinkler, and long summer evenings laughing around the barbecue. But she's exhausted. Carol's hoping that an evening at the beach will tire the kids out so she can have a nice quiet evening to herself.

After a few hours, the sun begins to set and the air becomes cooler. The kids have had a great time swimming, building sandcastles, running around the dunes and sword-fighting with driftwood, but now it's time to head home. Carol wrangles the kids and tells them to pack up and get in the car. After making sure everything and everyone is secure, she hops in, puts on her seatbelt, turns the key and looks in the rear-view mirror.

There she sees three kids, passed out, their heads resting on each other's shoulders. Nice one, Carol. Job done.

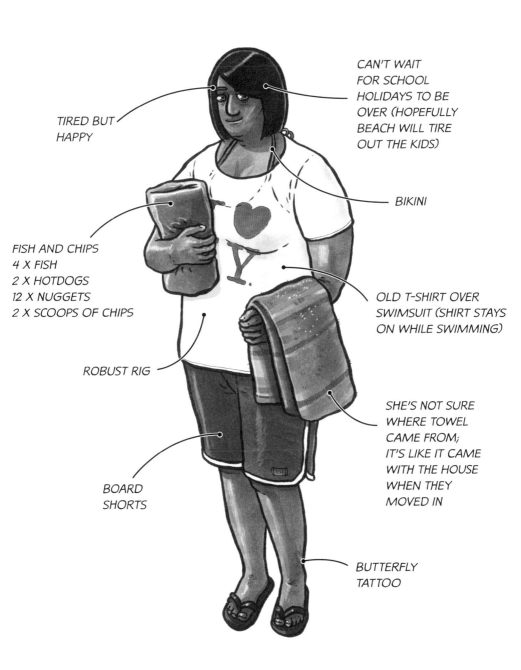

TIRED BUT HAPPY

CAN'T WAIT FOR SCHOOL HOLIDAYS TO BE OVER (HOPEFULLY BEACH WILL TIRE OUT THE KIDS)

BIKINI

FISH AND CHIPS
4 X FISH
2 X HOTDOGS
12 X NUGGETS
2 X SCOOPS OF CHIPS

OLD T-SHIRT OVER SWIMSUIT (SHIRT STAYS ON WHILE SWIMMING)

ROBUST RIG

SHE'S NOT SURE WHERE TOWEL CAME FROM; IT'S LIKE IT CAME WITH THE HOUSE WHEN THEY MOVED IN

BOARD SHORTS

BUTTERFLY TATTOO

CITY SHUFFLE JAXON

Jaxon isn't a bad kid; he just didn't really pay much attention in his final year of school. He's spent the past few months in limbo, not really sure what his next step is.

Most days he gets up around midday and takes the bus into town to meet up with his mates. From the bus exchange, they head to the supermarket to stock up on food and drink. Next up, they'll move on to the cinema or arcade to see what everyone else is doing. If nothing is going on they'll shuffle up the road to the food court and get $1 soft serves. They repeat this circuit until they find something interesting to do. Most of the time they find nothing.

Jaxon would never say this to his friends, but he's getting bored of bumming around doing nothing. He's started looking into doing a certificate in cookery at polytech. His Auntie Jan taught him how to cook years ago; it's something he really enjoys and one of the few activities where he feels genuinely confident.

Go on, Jaxon, sign up . . . you know you'll love it!

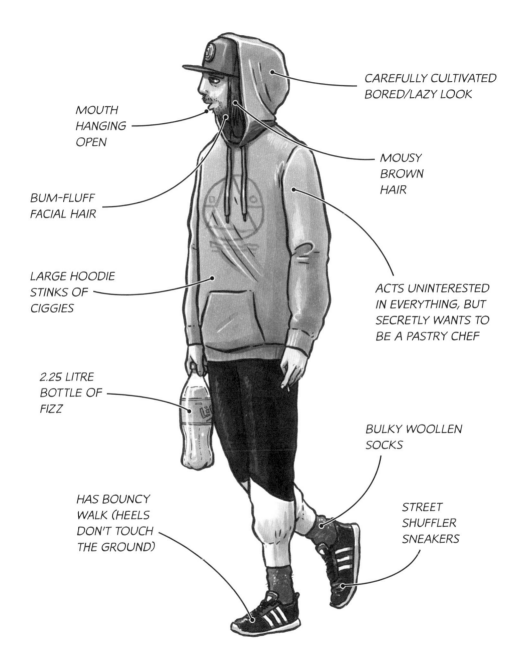

CAREFULLY CULTIVATED BORED/LAZY LOOK

MOUTH HANGING OPEN

MOUSY BROWN HAIR

BUM-FLUFF FACIAL HAIR

LARGE HOODIE STINKS OF CIGGIES

ACTS UNINTERESTED IN EVERYTHING, BUT SECRETLY WANTS TO BE A PASTRY CHEF

2.25 LITRE BOTTLE OF FIZZ

BULKY WOOLLEN SOCKS

HAS BOUNCY WALK (HEELS DON'T TOUCH THE GROUND)

STREET SHUFFLER SNEAKERS

EVENT SECURITY SHAAN

Shaan has one of the toughest jobs there is. Working security is a thankless job at the best of times, but at a sporting event it's almost unbearable. It's like being stone-cold sober at the biggest party of the year. He knows that everyone in the crowd wants to see him fall over chasing a streaker. He knows they're all just waiting for him to screw up so they can give him shit. He can't possibly win. He wants everyone to know that he used to be just like you and that he's just doing a job and following protocol . . . but you wouldn't understand.

Shaan can't wait until this is all over so he can take off his uniform and slip back into obscurity amongst the civilians. He focuses on his young family, his beautiful wife and daughter. They always get him through. The extra money he'll get over the summer will really help them: with any luck they'll even be able to go back home and visit his folks for the first time in years.

Stay positive, Shaan: focus on the end goal and you'll make it.

SLEEPY, DISINTERESTED FEATURES

HIVE MIND

LEARNED HATRED OF BEACH BALLS

PATCHY FACIAL HAIR

COMMON SENSE AND CRITICAL THINKING

POCKET CONTAINS KNIFE FOR POPPING INFLATABLES

STRUGGLING TO LOOK BUSY

JUST WANTS TO GO HOME

ENORMOUS JACKET

SHAPELESS PANTS

CHUNKY RUGGED SHARK SHOES

DEDICATED MUM JANET

Janet has done a fantastic job of the most difficult job there is: she's raised two boys into fantastic young men. Her elder son is doing great at uni down south and her younger boy is nearing the end of his final year at school, so she's cherishing every moment of school life. You can guarantee that if there's a school event, Janet will be there, clipping tickets, manning the barbecue or directing traffic in the car park.

There's nothing that this superwoman can't do.

She's not sure what she'll do when the boys are both away from home; maybe she'll finally go on that European cruise. Treat yourself, Janet: you deserve it.

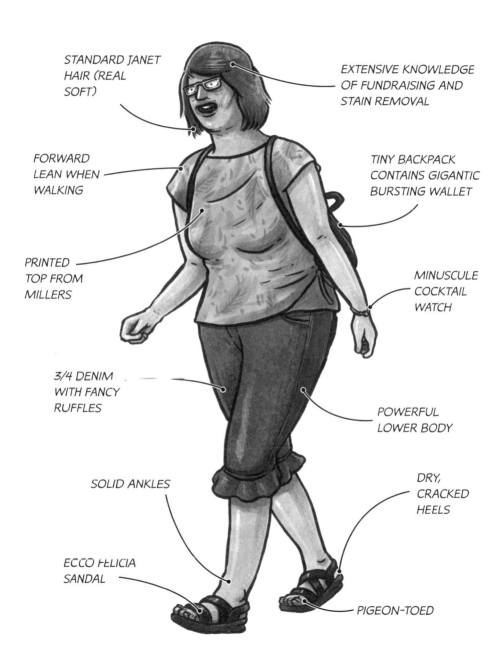

STANDARD JANET HAIR (REAL SOFT)

EXTENSIVE KNOWLEDGE OF FUNDRAISING AND STAIN REMOVAL

FORWARD LEAN WHEN WALKING

TINY BACKPACK CONTAINS GIGANTIC BURSTING WALLET

PRINTED TOP FROM MILLERS

MINUSCULE COCKTAIL WATCH

3/4 DENIM WITH FANCY RUFFLES

POWERFUL LOWER BODY

SOLID ANKLES

DRY, CRACKED HEELS

ECCO FELICIA SANDAL

PIGEON-TOED

PRESIDENT'S GRADE GAVIN

Gavin has a love-hate relationship with the gentleman's game. From Monday to Thursday he really looks forward to his Saturday long match. But when Friday arrives, he begins to wish for a wet weekend. He's just not sure he wants to spend his whole Saturday standing in the middle of a windy field next to a motorway. Sure, he loves cricket; but when he's out there he prays that no catches come his way (if he drops another one he'll never hear the end of it), and when he's batting he just wants to get off strike. But he knows he'll keep coming back week after week, summer after summer. He loves his team mates and there's nothing better than heading to the pub after the game to tell cricketing war stories over a pint and a pie. Cheers, Gavin, have a cold one on me.

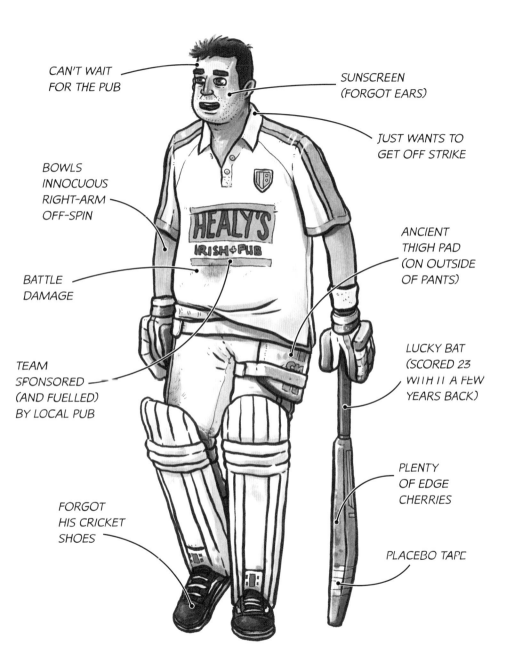

CAN'T WAIT FOR THE PUB

SUNSCREEN (FORGOT EARS)

JUST WANTS TO GET OFF STRIKE

BOWLS INNOCUOUS RIGHT-ARM OFF-SPIN

BATTLE DAMAGE

ANCIENT THIGH PAD (ON OUTSIDE OF PANTS)

TEAM SPONSORED (AND FUELLED) BY LOCAL PUB

LUCKY BAT (SCORED 23 WITH IT A FEW YEARS BACK)

FORGOT HIS CRICKET SHOES

PLENTY OF EDGE CHERRIES

PLACEBO TAPE

HEALY'S
IRISH+PUB

HYDRATING PERSON

Absolutely neutral Hydrating Person is the perfect being for those who get offended by drawings of fictional New Zealanders. Try not to get upset.

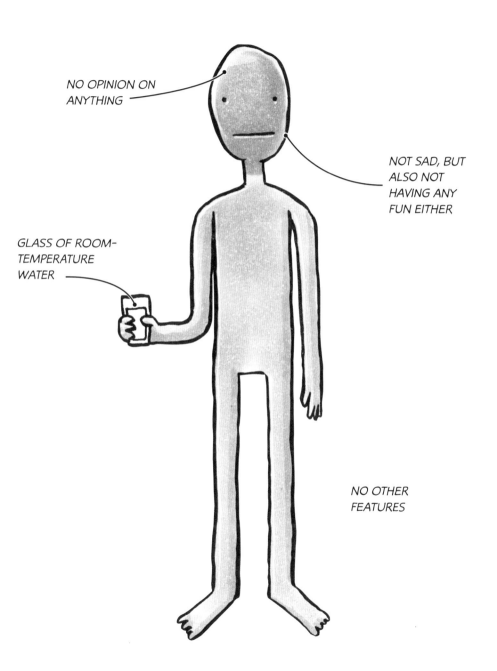

NO OPINION ON ANYTHING

NOT SAD, BUT ALSO NOT HAVING ANY FUN EITHER

GLASS OF ROOM-TEMPERATURE WATER

NO OTHER FEATURES

RACES AFTERMATH BECCA

Cup Day is Becca's favourite day of the year. She's got a new outfit (she'll wear it only once) and a new fascinator, all her friends are looking fabulous and, best of all, she knows someone working at the Lindauer bar, so she's guaranteed a few freebies throughout the course of the day. The whole horse thing doesn't really interest Becca: she just wants to hang out with her besties, make *weeeeoooo* noises when she hears a bottle of bubbles being opened and check out the male talent.

Have a great day, Becca; live, laugh, love, but be sure to pace yourself—you don't want to get on the news again this year!

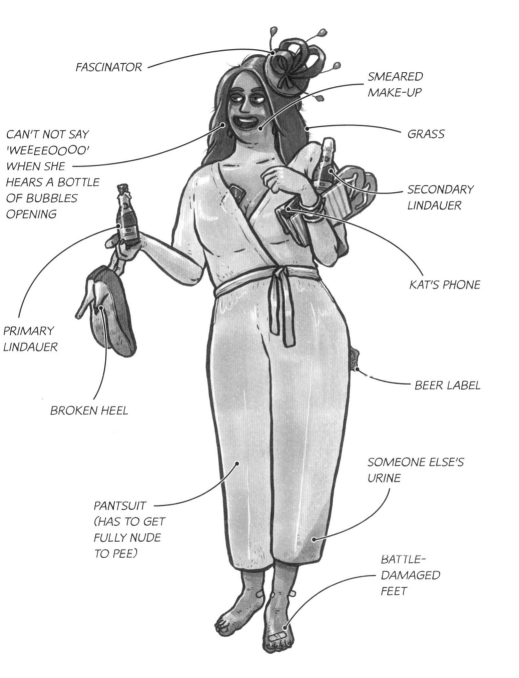

FASCINATOR

SMEARED MAKE-UP

GRASS

CAN'T NOT SAY 'WEEEEOOOO' WHEN SHE HEARS A BOTTLE OF BUBBLES OPENING

SECONDARY LINDAUER

KAT'S PHONE

PRIMARY LINDAUER

BEER LABEL

BROKEN HEEL

SOMEONE ELSE'S URINE

PANTSUIT (HAS TO GET FULLY NUDE TO PEE)

BATTLE-DAMAGED FEET

PARK STROLL KEN

Ken cherishes his daily stroll around the park. After decades of hard work running a successful restaurant and raising a large family, he finally has time for himself. He came to New Zealand with nothing and now has more than he could have ever imagined. Although he's supremely proud of the business empire he has built, nothing compares to the satisfaction he feels when surrounded by his family. His children have grown up to be great businesspeople and even better humans, and his grandchildren (although a little ill-disciplined) are beyond adorable.

When not enjoying the local park, Ken loves looking after his five grandchildren, hitting the driving range, perusing the real estate listings and napping in the car. Take it easy, Ken!

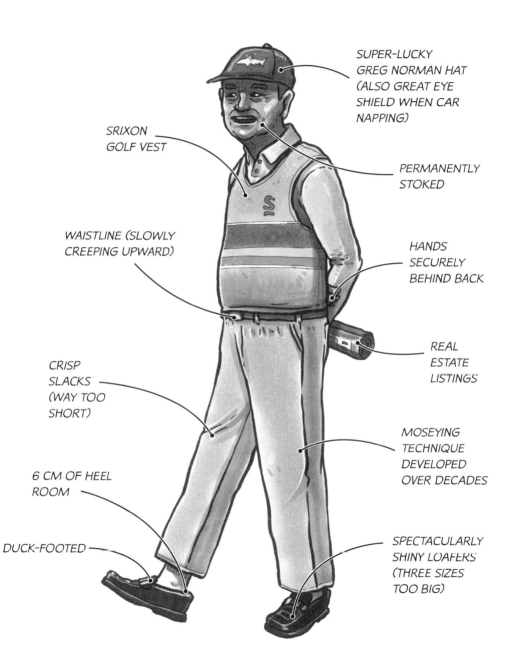

SUPER-LUCKY GREG NORMAN HAT (ALSO GREAT EYE SHIELD WHEN CAR NAPPING)

SRIXON GOLF VEST

PERMANENTLY STOKED

WAISTLINE (SLOWLY CREEPING UPWARD)

HANDS SECURELY BEHIND BACK

REAL ESTATE LISTINGS

CRISP SLACKS (WAY TOO SHORT)

MOSEYING TECHNIQUE DEVELOPED OVER DECADES

6 CM OF HEEL ROOM

DUCK-FOOTED

SPECTACULARLY SHINY LOAFERS (THREE SIZES TOO BIG)

WILL
THE
SUIT

Will had always wanted to be a businessman. When he was a young lad he'd always make sure he was up early to see his dad before he left for work. Would he be wearing the grey double-breasted suit, or would it be his favourite dark blue number? Will loved to watch him read the business pages of the paper as he sipped his morning coffee; he had no idea what the facts and figures meant, but it seemed really important to his dad.

The biggest mystery, though, was his dad's briefcase. It was a deep brown leather case with gold rotary locks and latches. He loved the sound it made when his dad unlocked it. But what was in there? Top-secret codes? Bundles of cash? His Christmas wish-list?

Today, Will has his own briefcase. He doesn't really need it and it rarely contains anything of importance, but it makes him feel good as he carries it through the front door at work each morning—and really, that's all that matters.

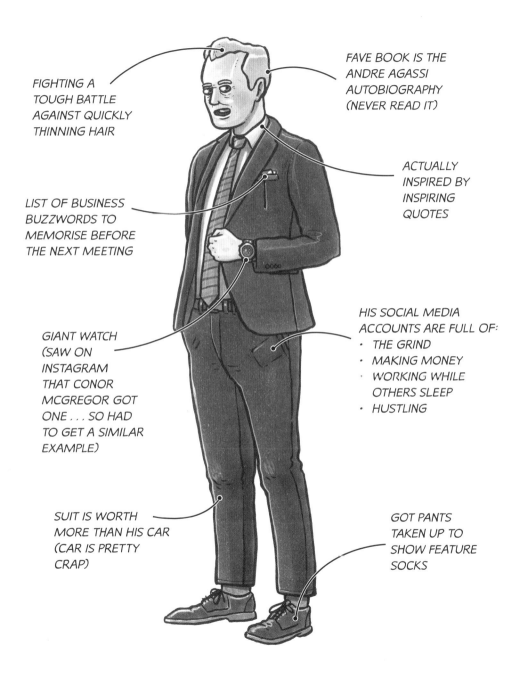

FIGHTING A TOUGH BATTLE AGAINST QUICKLY THINNING HAIR

FAVE BOOK IS THE ANDRE AGASSI AUTOBIOGRAPHY (NEVER READ IT)

ACTUALLY INSPIRED BY INSPIRING QUOTES

LIST OF BUSINESS BUZZWORDS TO MEMORISE BEFORE THE NEXT MEETING

GIANT WATCH (SAW ON INSTAGRAM THAT CONOR MCGREGOR GOT ONE . . . SO HAD TO GET A SIMILAR EXAMPLE)

HIS SOCIAL MEDIA ACCOUNTS ARE FULL OF:
· THE GRIND
· MAKING MONEY
· WORKING WHILE OTHERS SLEEP
· HUSTLING

SUIT IS WORTH MORE THAN HIS CAR (CAR IS PRETTY CRAP)

GOT PANTS TAKEN UP TO SHOW FEATURE SOCKS

WORKSHOP TAMMY

Tammy is an absolute institution down at the workshop, and people aren't joking when they say the place would fall apart without her: she took two weeks off a few years ago and part of the shop roof caved in.

She knows the business like the back of her hand. Ask her to locate the order form for the 2005 Volkswagen Golf door handles and she can pick it out in an instant. Need the phone number for Les who came in three weeks ago? She knows it off the top of her head.

Don't tell the boys out back, but she earns way more than they do and the boss thinks she's worth every penny. He's no idiot: he knows who's in charge around here.

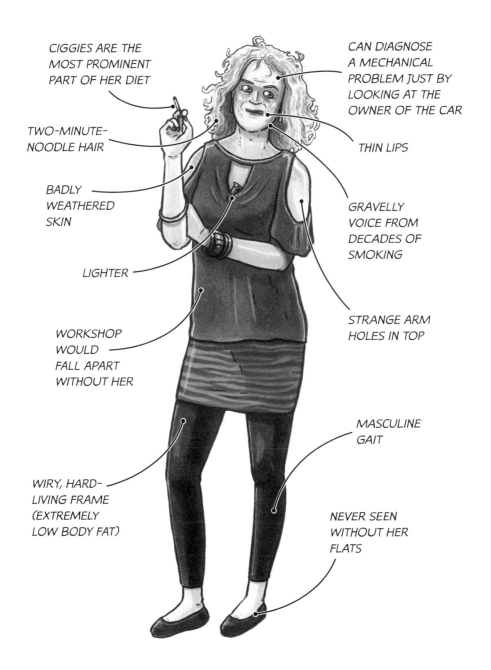

CIGGIES ARE THE MOST PROMINENT PART OF HER DIET

CAN DIAGNOSE A MECHANICAL PROBLEM JUST BY LOOKING AT THE OWNER OF THE CAR

TWO-MINUTE-NOODLE HAIR

THIN LIPS

BADLY WEATHERED SKIN

GRAVELLY VOICE FROM DECADES OF SMOKING

LIGHTER

WORKSHOP WOULD FALL APART WITHOUT HER

STRANGE ARM HOLES IN TOP

MASCULINE GAIT

WIRY, HARD-LIVING FRAME (EXTREMELY LOW BODY FAT)

NEVER SEEN WITHOUT HER FLATS

IMPORT-EXPORT TONY

Tony's lost count of the jobs he's had over the years, but he'll always remember his first. When he was 12 he worked at the dairy down the road from his mum's house. He loved that job. He'd take the expired lollies and chocolate bars from out the back and sell them to the kids at school the next day. He made a pretty tidy sum from doing that, but the real money was in magazines. There was always a huge demand for nudie magazines at school and he was the sole supplier.

This side-hustle made him pretty popular with his peers, as he always had money for the movies, arcade or Macca's and was never shy about sharing his wealth around.

In high school Tony found a job washing and detailing cars at one of the local yards. Impressed by his work ethic and personable manner, the owner decided to give him a chance on the sales floor. He was a natural and soon topped the company sales charts with ease.

After decades in the used-car business, Tony felt like a new challenge. He'd been holidaying in Bali for years and had some great local contacts, so it made sense to try to do business there.

Today, Tony imports rattan furniture from Indonesia. In 10 years he's grown from running one small location by himself to having 135 staff and 12 locations throughout the North Island. He's really enjoying himself at the moment, but he's always looking for a new challenge or opportunity. Tony has no idea where the business life will take him next, and that's just the way he likes it. Nice one, Tones!

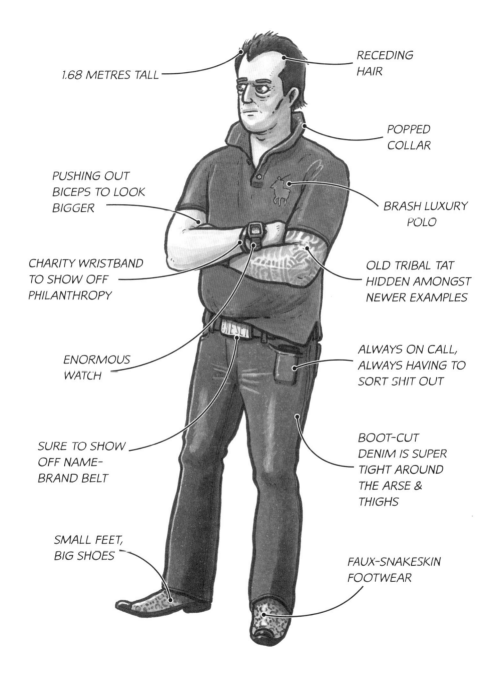

1.68 METRES TALL

RECEDING HAIR

POPPED COLLAR

PUSHING OUT BICEPS TO LOOK BIGGER

BRASH LUXURY POLO

CHARITY WRISTBAND TO SHOW OFF PHILANTHROPY

OLD TRIBAL TAT HIDDEN AMONGST NEWER EXAMPLES

ENORMOUS WATCH

ALWAYS ON CALL, ALWAYS HAVING TO SORT SHIT OUT

SURE TO SHOW OFF NAME-BRAND BELT

BOOT-CUT DENIM IS SUPER TIGHT AROUND THE ARSE & THIGHS

SMALL FEET, BIG SHOES

FAUX-SNAKESKIN FOOTWEAR

RETIRED GP SIMON

Initially, retirement wasn't easy for Simon. He loved his work and his colleagues, but he knew it was time to slow down.

In the beginning, he just didn't know what to do with himself. If there was no sport on television he was lost; he spent most of his time driving his poor wife Emily crazy.

But then Emily reminded him of something. When they first met, he'd been close to buying his dream yacht: a 37-ft Huromic Cutter. But then life happened, the kids were born, work got busier and busier and, before he knew it, almost 30 years had passed by. They had been an amazing 30 years, full of love and happiness, but now Simon had time to focus on himself.

He managed to find the perfect yacht on Trade Me. It needed a bit of work, but that's what he wanted: something that he could put some time and elbow grease into. Simon reckons he'll have the yacht seaworthy in about six months and is already planning a trip through the Bay of Islands next summer. If that goes well, he's going to try to convince Emily to sail with him to Fiji. Good luck with that, Simon!

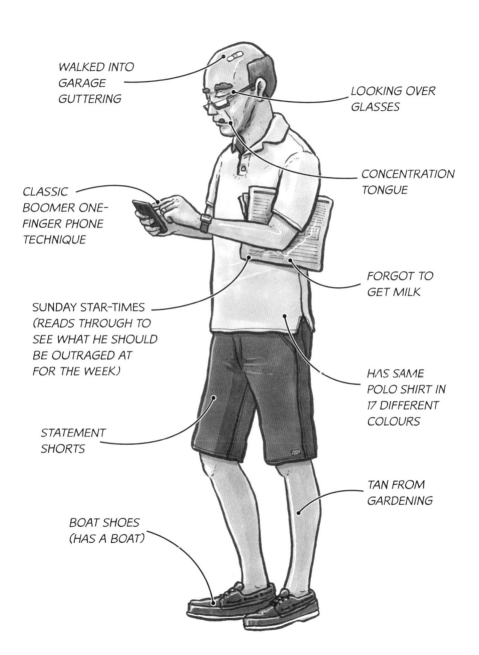

WALKED INTO GARAGE GUTTERING

LOOKING OVER GLASSES

CONCENTRATION TONGUE

CLASSIC BOOMER ONE-FINGER PHONE TECHNIQUE

FORGOT TO GET MILK

SUNDAY STAR-TIMES (READS THROUGH TO SEE WHAT HE SHOULD BE OUTRAGED AT FOR THE WEEK)

HAS SAME POLO SHIRT IN 17 DIFFERENT COLOURS

STATEMENT SHORTS

TAN FROM GARDENING

BOAT SHOES (HAS A BOAT)

TAKAKA
GATHERING
SKYE

Skye wasn't always the most spiritual person growing up—in fact, she'd never really had any interest in that sort of thing at all. Looking back on it now, it all seems so strange to Skye; her new life is so different.

It seems like a lifetime ago, but she can still remember as clear as day when everything changed.

She'd heard about Ecstasy before but had never looked into it. Her best friend Stacey had done it before and asked if she was interested. She was a little hesitant, but she trusted her friend and thought she'd give it a try. She took the pill and lay down on her bed next to Stacey.

After about 30 minutes she started to feel something. She felt warm and relaxed, as though she was being enveloped in love and peacefulness. Her mind was so clear, every problem had a solution, every negative thought turned into something positive, and she felt connected to everything and everyone. It was amazing . . . it was life-changing.

After that moment Skye was a different person. Her priorities had changed in an instant. Work was no longer her focus: being happy was all that mattered. She sold almost everything she had, bought a campervan and moved to Nelson. She spends the summers travelling the countryside with her rescue dog Blue, picking up just enough work to keep her van fuelled and her body fed. You're living the dream, Skye!

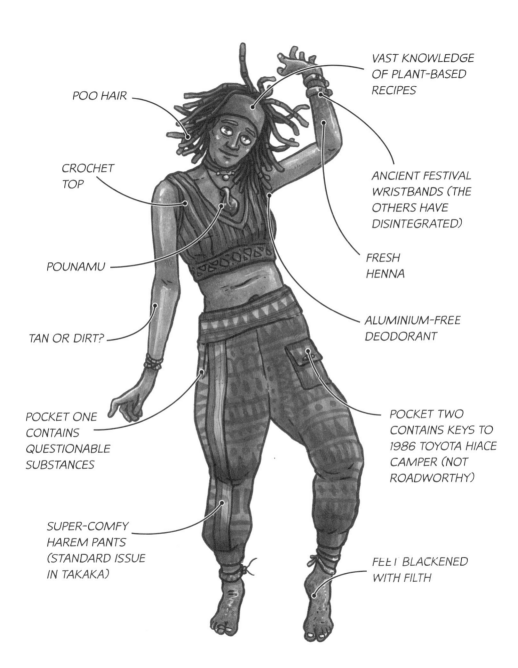

POO HAIR

VAST KNOWLEDGE OF PLANT-BASED RECIPES

CROCHET TOP

ANCIENT FESTIVAL WRISTBANDS (THE OTHERS HAVE DISINTEGRATED)

POUNAMU

FRESH HENNA

TAN OR DIRT?

ALUMINIUM-FREE DEODORANT

POCKET ONE CONTAINS QUESTIONABLE SUBSTANCES

POCKET TWO CONTAINS KEYS TO 1986 TOYOTA HIACE CAMPER (NOT ROADWORTHY)

SUPER-COMFY HAREM PANTS (STANDARD ISSUE IN TAKAKA)

FEET BLACKENED WITH FILTH

REFORMED RHYS

Twenty years ago, if you'd told Rhys that he'd have the life that he has now he would have laughed in your face, then probably punched you in the face. Rhys is the first to admit that he wasn't a great guy back then. He mixed with the wrong people and he got into a lot of trouble. He doesn't like to talk about his time in prison; he just wants to forget about that part of his life, because he's a different person now.

Rhys's life began to change after his mum died. It helped him put things into perspective and it made him realise that he couldn't keep living his life the way he was living it. He got a bit of money from the sale of his mum's house and he used it to buy a tow truck so he could start his own towing business. Two decades on and the business is thriving: he's got 15 trucks, two locations and 25 staff. He never thought he'd say this, but he loves going into work each day.

Work might be going great, but home life is the thing that really makes Rhys happy. His wife has supported him through everything and he honestly believes he'd be dead if he hadn't met her. Rhys recently found out that he's going to be a granddad; it was a shock at first but he's slowly coming to grips with the idea. Don't worry, Rhys, you'll do fine.

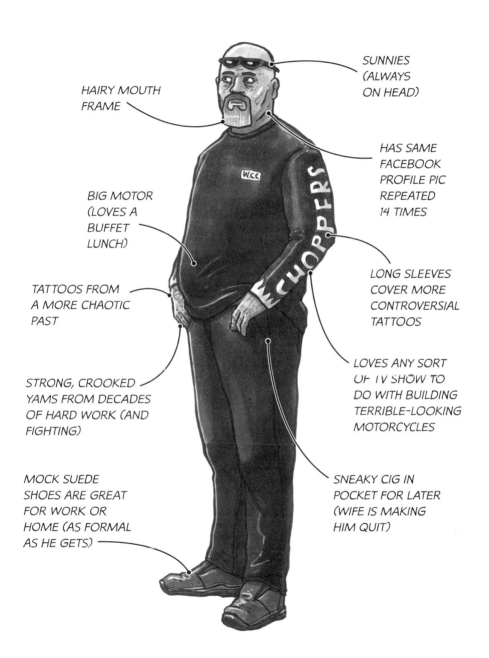

SUNNIES (ALWAYS ON HEAD)

HAIRY MOUTH FRAME

HAS SAME FACEBOOK PROFILE PIC REPEATED 14 TIMES

BIG MOTOR (LOVES A BUFFET LUNCH)

W.C.R

CHOPPERS

LONG SLEEVES COVER MORE CONTROVERSIAL TATTOOS

TATTOOS FROM A MORE CHAOTIC PAST

LOVES ANY SORT OF TV SHOW TO DO WITH BUILDING TERRIBLE-LOOKING MOTORCYCLES

STRONG, CROOKED YAMS FROM DECADES OF HARD WORK (AND FIGHTING)

MOCK SUEDE SHOES ARE GREAT FOR WORK OR HOME (AS FORMAL AS HE GETS)

SNEAKY CIG IN POCKET FOR LATER (WIFE IS MAKING HIM QUIT)

AIRPORT TAXI RON

Ron has spent the best part of 20 years ferrying people around the city. Although the hours can be tough, he loves the social aspect of his job and is alway up for a good chat about current events or the weather. Prior to becoming a taxi driver, Ron spent 22 years in the police force, rising to the rank of sergeant before retiring, so he knows how to deal with unruly passengers. When not driving, Ron loves playing with his grandchildren and tending to his expansive garden (his mates say he has the nicest lawn-edging in the whole suburb).

Remember, guys and girls: always thank the driver at the end of your journey!

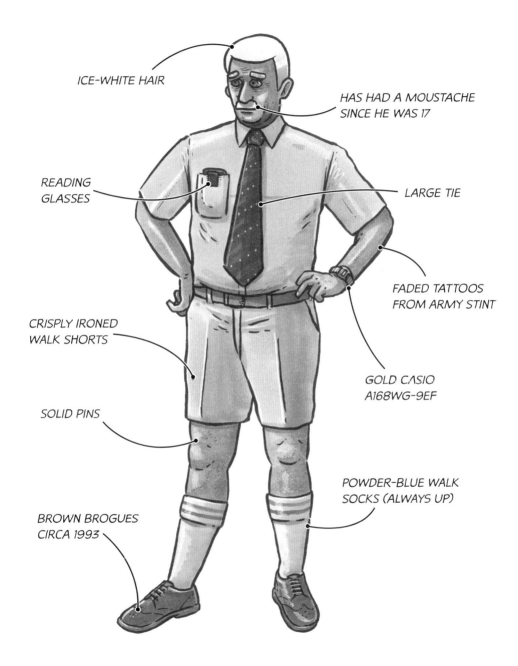

ICE-WHITE HAIR

HAS HAD A MOUSTACHE
SINCE HE WAS 17

READING
GLASSES

LARGE TIE

FADED TATTOOS
FROM ARMY STINT

CRISPLY IRONED
WALK SHORTS

GOLD CASIO
A168WG-9EF

SOLID PINS

POWDER-BLUE WALK
SOCKS (ALWAYS UP)

BROWN BROGUES
CIRCA 1993

EXPEDITION MAVIS

Mavis is an interesting sight as she shuffles down the busy main road on her almost daily expedition to the shopping mall. It takes about 50 minutes for her to make the epic journey but she absolutely loves it.

She loves the fresh air, the exercise and waving to people (regardless of whether she knows them or not) as they go by. The doctor told her to take it easy for a while after she rolled her ankle, but she insists that he doesn't know what he's talking about.

The staff at the Muffin Break in the mall all know Mavis; it's a little annoying when she holds everyone up during the lunchtime rush by insisting on paying with exact change, but they still love seeing her totter on up every day.

She won't be heading to the mall tomorrow, though, as her eldest son Iain is taking her to the casino for a buffet lunch with the extended family. She can't wait! Don't go too hard, Mavis!

RISKING LIFE AND LIMB GOING FOR A WAVE

SAYS HELLO TO EVERYONE

ALWAYS RUGGED UP

BEIGE IS HER FAVOURITE COLOUR

A LITTLE RACIST

TRIP TO THE MALL WILL TAKE ALL DAY

RAPIDLY SHRINKING BODY

BADLY SWOLLEN ANKLE

SHOP ROLLER 6300 EXECUTIVE (CALLS IT 'ROGER')

MAGS

LARGE SLIPPERS FOR STREET SHUFFLING

KORU LOUNGE REGAN

Today Regan's off to Sydney for a business meeting. Regan loves going on business trips: not for the business, but for the travel. He's only a few points away from qualifying for Gold status on his Koru membership and if he gets that he reckons he can make a big push for Gold Elite in the next 12 months or so.

Although his flight isn't until 8.25 a.m., Regan's made sure that he's at the airport super early as he hates having to wait in line at customs. A bonus for getting there early is that he gets to spend some quality time in the Koru Lounge. He loves it there. The first thing he does when he arrives is get a good seat: private but with a good view of the buffet, so he can see any new treats being added to the selection. Next up, he makes sure all of his devices have successfully logged on to the wi-fi, then it's off to get food and drink. First off he loads up on the breakfast option of sausages, Mexican-style breakfast beans and bright golden-yellow scrambled eggs. By the time he's returned to his seat his large flat white is ready (ordered on the app on the way through the duty-free area), so he's all set. Over the next few hours he'll have many more coffees and make another half-dozen trips back to the buffet. Nice one, Regan: it sounds like the perfect way to start your trip.

WARY OF ANYONE IN LOUNGE UNDER 35 OR WITH TATTOOS

FIRST PLATE OF FOOD (GOT TO AIRPORT EARLY FOR CROSSOVER BETWEEN BREAKFAST AND LUNCH)

DREAMS OF GOLD ELITE STATUS

WILL HAVE SELECTION OF CHEESE AND CRACKERS AFTER MAIN MEAL

BODY-HUGGING ICEBREAKER TOP

ALL GADGETS SYNCHED

CRISP DENIM

BAG CONTAINS:
· LAPTOP
· VARIOUS CORDS AND CHARGERS
· TOP GEAR MAGAZINE

SMART-CASUAL SHOES

PHONE
CHAT
NISHAN

When Nishan first arrived in New Zealand he was shocked. He knew it wasn't going to be anything like his home of Gurugram in northern India, but this was crazy. Actually, it was very much un-crazy. Where were the people? Where were the cars? Had he arrived during an air raid or something? Was everyone hiding in bomb shelters?

Eight years later and Nishan's grown to love the slower pace of life and open spaces of his adopted home. He still struggles with the cold weather a little, but he can't think of a better place to bring up his young family. He's just been on the phone to his mum and dad back home. After years of trying, he's finally convinced them to make the big trip over to New Zealand. His parents have never met his two young boys so he's beyond excited about them arriving. Say hi to them for us, Nishan!

THICK, LUSCIOUS HAIR

LOVES TALKING ON THE PHONE OUTSIDE (FOR HOURS AT A TIME)

VARIOUS FABRIC BRACELETS AND STRAPS

SHIRT HAS STRANGE DETAILING

FAVOURS A BUTTON-UP SHIRT

WATCH WITH FAT LEATHER STRAP

JEANS WITH ELABORATE DETAILING AND DISTRESSING

LANYARD ATTACHED TO KEYS OF 2000 FORD LASER (STANDARD APART FROM ENORMOUS EXHAUST)

ALWAYS WEARS SANDALS (EVEN IN SUB-ZERO TEMPERATURES)

SATURDAY MARKET NORA

This is Nora's favourite time of the week. She gets up early, puts on her browsing sandals, grabs her satchel and heads down to the local market. She's got a list of things she needs but she knows she'll probably come back with a few unexpected treasures.

First up, she's on the lookout for a nice fresh ciabatta for lunch— and will she pick up some of that free-range prosciutto to go with it? Yes, that'll do perfectly; Jim (her husband) will love tucking into that after an arduous morning mowing the lawns. Next, she needs to find something to take to Jan's place for afternoon tea. Maybe a tasty chutney or blue cheese?

It's not just the produce that she loves: the people are great, too. She loves to stop and have a chat with the owners of her favourite stalls and they're always so happy to yarn and give advice.

Enjoy the rest of your weekend, Nora!

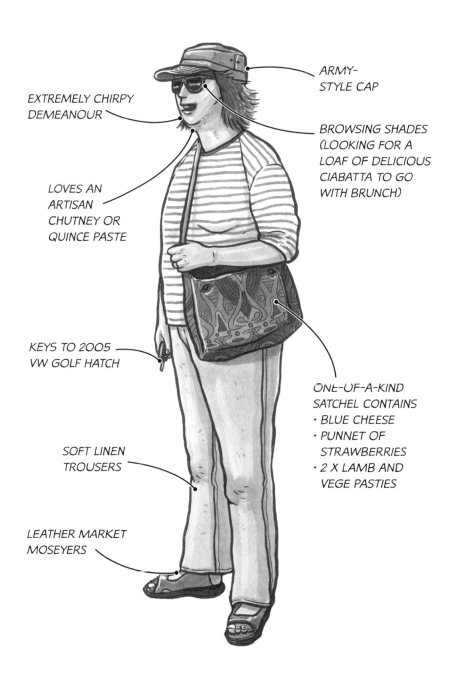

EXTREMELY CHIRPY
DEMEANOUR

ARMY-
STYLE CAP

BROWSING SHADES
(LOOKING FOR A
LOAF OF DELICIOUS
CIABATTA TO GO
WITH BRUNCH)

LOVES AN
ARTISAN
CHUTNEY OR
QUINCE PASTE

KEYS TO 2005
VW GOLF HATCH

ONE-OF-A-KIND
SATCHEL CONTAINS
· BLUE CHEESE
· PUNNET OF
  STRAWBERRIES
· 2 X LAMB AND
  VEGE PASTIES

SOFT LINEN
TROUSERS

LEATHER MARKET
MOSEYERS

FORMAL MORRIS

Morris can't remember the last time he went to an event like this. Was it his sister's second wedding in '94? Maybe it was baby Martin's christening? Either way, he hasn't worn a tie in decades.

Morris may feel a little like a fish out of water, but he's absolutely stoked to be invited to his nephew's engagement party. There are so many familiar faces that he hasn't seen in years. Auntie Colleen's looking so old, and little Jesse isn't little anymore! Has it really been that long since he caught up with everyone?

Morris thinks how silly he was feeling nervous about coming along tonight, grabs another club sandwich and heads to the bar.

Have a good one, Morris!

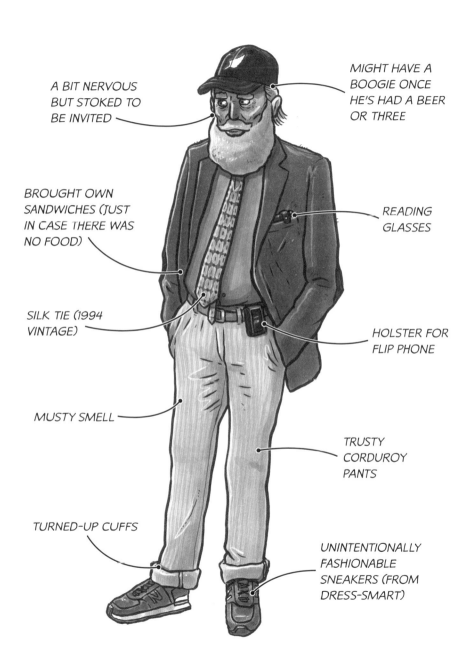

A BIT NERVOUS BUT STOKED TO BE INVITED

MIGHT HAVE A BOOGIE ONCE HE'S HAD A BEER OR THREE

BROUGHT OWN SANDWICHES (JUST IN CASE THERE WAS NO FOOD)

READING GLASSES

SILK TIE (1994 VINTAGE)

HOLSTER FOR FLIP PHONE

MUSTY SMELL

TRUSTY CORDUROY PANTS

TURNED-UP CUFFS

UNINTENTIONALLY FASHIONABLE SNEAKERS (FROM DRESS-SMART)

TATTOO ARTIST MASON

Mason's parents have always been super supportive of his creative endeavours, and if he's shown interest in something, they've always done their best to help him achieve his goals.

When he was younger he was into everything hiphop-related, so they made sure he had the best decks and equipment and access to a great DJing coach.

By his late teens he'd become obsessed with graphic design and illustration, so they fully supported him when he decided to embark on a design degree.

During his second year at uni he discovered tattoos, and after his friend gave him a few stick-and-poke examples he was hooked: he had to try to make a career out of it. He dropped out of the degree and managed to find someone willing to give him an apprenticeship—and, as they say, the rest is history.

Today (with the help of his parents) Mason is the owner of his own tattoo studio. He's having a great time, surrounded by amazingly talented people. But Mason doesn't stand still for long: he's already close to releasing his first line of t-shirts and he thinks he might convert the back room into a recording studio.

CYCLING-STYLE CAP

RAY-BANS

FASHIONABLE MO

DOESN'T LIKE
SMOKING BUT
EVERYONE ELSE IN
THE SHOP DOES IT

EARLY (BADLY
DONE) TATS
HIDDEN UNDER
SHIRT

WISHES HIS
UPBRINGING
WAS WORSE SO
HE'D HAVE MORE
STREET CRED

PRISTINE SKATE TEE
(WOULD LOVE TO
BE A SKATER BUT
HAS ZERO ABILITY)

LEAN FRAME

TRUSTY
WELL-WORN
VANS

CRISP WHITE
ATHLETIC SOCKS

AUNTIE LENA

Everyone knows Auntie Lena, and it doesn't matter if you're related to her or not: everyone calls her Auntie. Nobody remembers a time when Auntie Lena wasn't around; it's like she came with the town.

Auntie Lena's door is always open—spend more than half an hour at her house and there's bound to be at least one person popping in for a chat and a cup of tea (she thinks her record is 23 cuppas in one day). When the local school wanted to organise a fundraising fireworks night, the first person they went to was Auntie Lena. They knew she'd know someone who could help them out, and they weren't wrong.

If Auntie Lena worked in the corporate world she'd be the CEO of a multi-million-dollar event-management company, but that's not her style.

She just loves her town and she loves her community. Bless you, Auntie Lena, we don't deserve you.

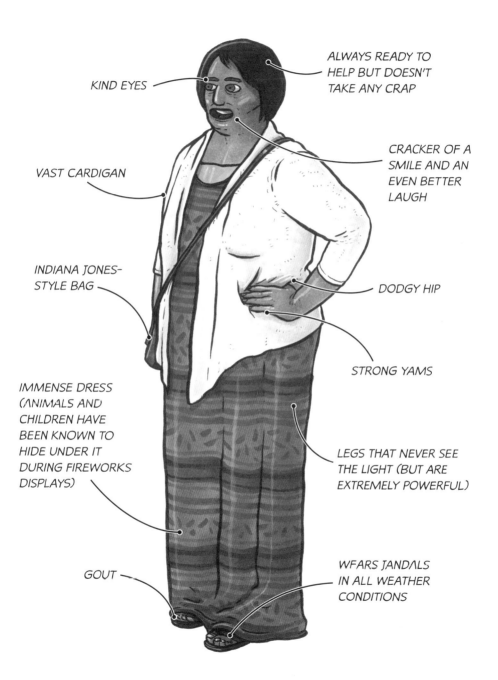

KIND EYES

ALWAYS READY TO HELP BUT DOESN'T TAKE ANY CRAP

CRACKER OF A SMILE AND AN EVEN BETTER LAUGH

VAST CARDIGAN

INDIANA JONES-STYLE BAG

DODGY HIP

STRONG YAMS

IMMENSE DRESS (ANIMALS AND CHILDREN HAVE BEEN KNOWN TO HIDE UNDER IT DURING FIREWORKS DISPLAYS)

LEGS THAT NEVER SEE THE LIGHT (BUT ARE EXTREMELY POWERFUL)

GOUT

WEARS JANDALS IN ALL WEATHER CONDITIONS

STREET SHUFFLER LES

The highlight of Les's day is his 90-minute, 200-metre journey down to the shops to buy the daily paper and some milk. He doesn't really need milk, but he uses it as an excuse to get out of the house each morning. All going well, he'll bump into the usual characters along the way and chat about the weather and the state of the roads—and if he's lucky, someone might ask him for directions!

Once home, Les makes a fresh brew, cracks open the Scotch Fingers and settles down in his favourite chair to while away the morning listening to Newstalk ZB.

Rest up, Les, you've earned it.

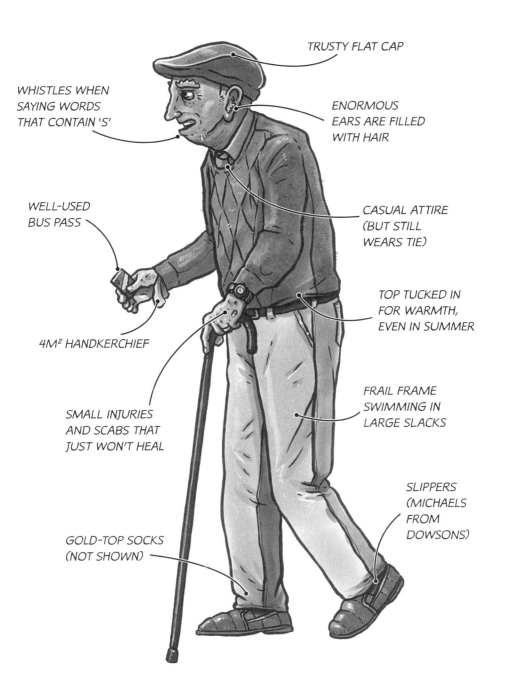

TRUSTY FLAT CAP

WHISTLES WHEN SAYING WORDS THAT CONTAIN 'S'

ENORMOUS EARS ARE FILLED WITH HAIR

WELL-USED BUS PASS

CASUAL ATTIRE (BUT STILL WEARS TIE)

TOP TUCKED IN FOR WARMTH, EVEN IN SUMMER

4M² HANDKERCHIEF

FRAIL FRAME SWIMMING IN LARGE SLACKS

SMALL INJURIES AND SCABS THAT JUST WON'T HEAL

SLIPPERS (MICHAELS FROM DOWSONS)

GOLD-TOP SOCKS (NOT SHOWN)

AGENCY OWNER LIAM

Things were very different back in 1994 when Liam began work in the creative industry. He started as a graphic designer at a local advertising agency and over the next few years moved up through the ranks to art director, then on to senior creative and now agency owner.

Back in the day, all you needed to have a successful ad campaign was a half-decent idea and enough budget to get that idea in front of as many eyeballs as possible. He misses those days.

Things are a little more complicated now. He has to worry about things like deliverables, impressions, brand funnels and something called geotargeting. Luckily for Liam, he now employs a bunch of people who know exactly what those things are.

He may not understand everything that's happening around him, but Liam's creative experience, personality and way with people are an invaluable asset to the company—and remember, it's *his* company, so he can do what he wants!

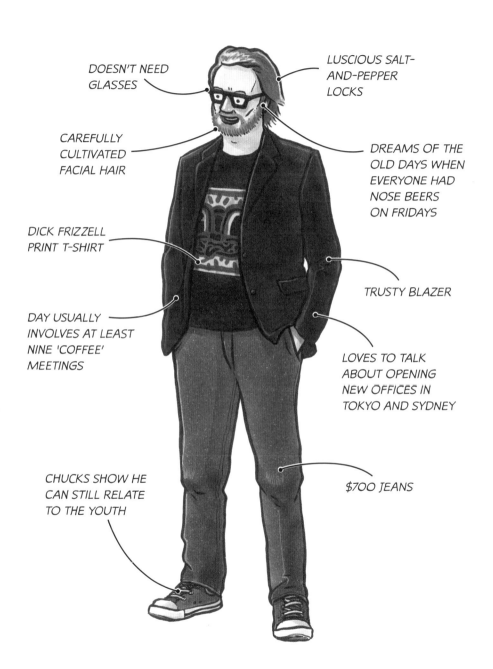

DOESN'T NEED
GLASSES

LUSCIOUS SALT-
AND-PEPPER
LOCKS

CAREFULLY
CULTIVATED
FACIAL HAIR

DREAMS OF THE
OLD DAYS WHEN
EVERYONE HAD
NOSE BEERS
ON FRIDAYS

DICK FRIZZELL
PRINT T-SHIRT

TRUSTY BLAZER

DAY USUALLY
INVOLVES AT LEAST
NINE 'COFFEE'
MEETINGS

LOVES TO TALK
ABOUT OPENING
NEW OFFICES IN
TOKYO AND SYDNEY

CHUCKS SHOW HE
CAN STILL RELATE
TO THE YOUTH

$700 JEANS

NURSE NGAIRE

Ngaire's just passed the halfway mark of her 12-hour shift and is heading to the hospital café to get her third coffee of the day.

Some people think that all nurses do is clean up patient messes, rotate the odd old person and do whatever the doctor tells them to do. Those people have obviously never spent more than five minutes in a hospital. On any given day Ngaire could be administering medication, dressing wounds, subtly assessing a patient's mental state or diagnosing a deadly condition.

Next time you see Ngaire waiting in line at the café, offer to buy her a brew: you never know when you might need her services.

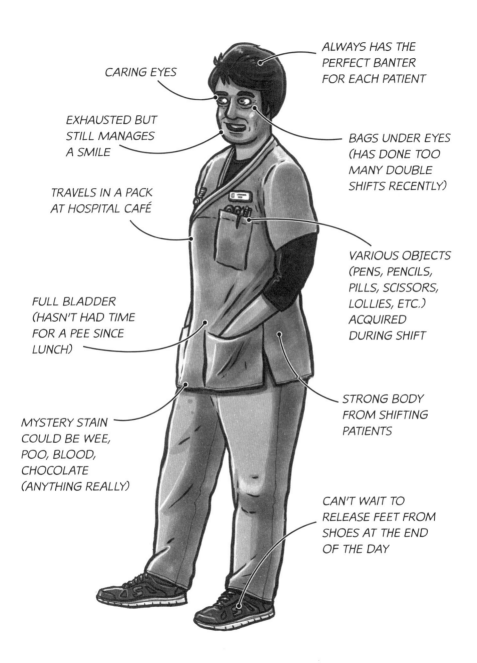

CARING EYES

ALWAYS HAS THE PERFECT BANTER FOR EACH PATIENT

EXHAUSTED BUT STILL MANAGES A SMILE

BAGS UNDER EYES (HAS DONE TOO MANY DOUBLE SHIFTS RECENTLY)

TRAVELS IN A PACK AT HOSPITAL CAFÉ

VARIOUS OBJECTS (PENS, PENCILS, PILLS, SCISSORS, LOLLIES, ETC.) ACQUIRED DURING SHIFT

FULL BLADDER (HASN'T HAD TIME FOR A PEE SINCE LUNCH)

STRONG BODY FROM SHIFTING PATIENTS

MYSTERY STAIN COULD BE WEE, POO, BLOOD, CHOCOLATE (ANYTHING REALLY)

CAN'T WAIT TO RELEASE FEET FROM SHOES AT THE END OF THE DAY

LUNCHTIME RAY

After a bad knee injury put an end to his representative rugby league career, Ray was devastated. He loved the camaraderie that the game provided, and it had been such a big part of his life for so long. He didn't really know what to do with himself.

After months of stagnation, Ray could feel the black dog of depression creeping over him. He knew he had to do something: he had to get back out there, set new goals and live his life with purpose again.

A few of the older guys at his club had been working in construction during the off-season, so he asked if there was any work available. Luckily for him, there was plenty. Right from the start, Ray was the perfect employee. He turned up on time, was eager to learn and listened to instructions, so he needed to be shown how to do something only once.

Ray's loving the work. The physical side is great, he's learning something new every day and, best of all, his workmates are awesome. Go, Ray!

GREAT LEAGUE CHAT

HARD HAT BALANCING ON TOP OF HEAD (NEVER PROPERLY SECURED)

POWERFUL FRAME (GOOD AT MOST SPORTS)

HARD-WORKING YAMS

LUNCH:
· 2 X WHOPPERS
· 2 X LARGE FRIES
· 6 X NUGGETS (YOUNG ENOUGH THAT THIS WON'T MAKE HIM FAT)

KEYS TO WORK UTE

DICKIES WORK SHORTS

QUALITY TATTOOS LINK HIM TO HIS HERITAGE

WALK
OF SHAME
WADE

Wade had a bloody good night last night—well, the parts he can recall seemed pretty fun anyway. There's a bit of a murky spot in there somewhere involving a shopping trolley and a road cone, but he definitely remembers the final part of the evening.

Kylie had been dropping hints about him coming over for weeks but he wasn't super confident around girls, especially ones he really liked. Still, with the help of their friends (who'd purposely left them together) and a little Dutch courage, he'd finally managed to tell her how he felt; he was pretty stoked with himself, to be honest.

That feeling of happiness almost masked the dustiness of his hangover. But his mouth was dry, his head was beginning to throb and his guts were rumbling: he needed pie and electrolyte-based medical attention ASAP! Luckily for Wade, the servo was only a 10-minute walk away, so he could buy what he needed. Hopefully he can grab a taxi and get home before Mum gets up to do the weekly grocery shop. Godspeed, young Wade!

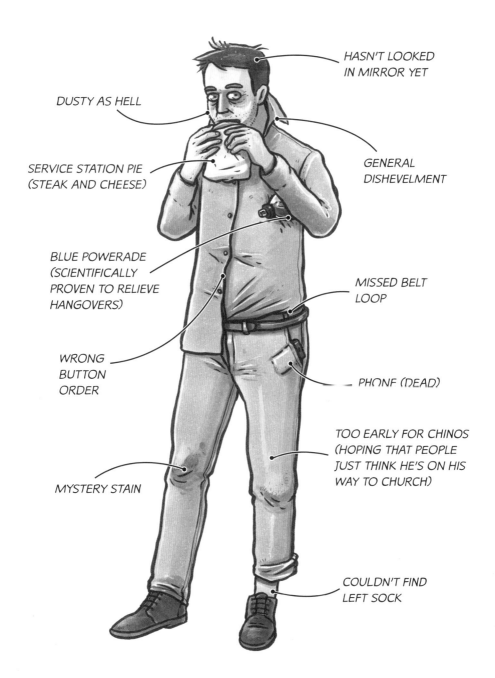

SCHOOL COUNSELLOR AJA

Aja was born to be a counsellor. She has a special way with people: they love her and she loves them. She's been working at her current school for almost 10 years and she's never met a kid she couldn't help.

Some of the children at her school aren't from the most privileged backgrounds, so sometimes her job can be tough, especially when dealing with stubborn parents who are stuck in their ways. But these challenges are what make her job so rewarding. Recently one of her old students came to visit her after a few years out of school. He was an intelligent kid who struggled to focus, but with her help he passed his university entrance exams and is now thriving. It makes it all worthwhile.

After years of focusing on others, Aja is now trying to get a better work-life balance. She's started eating better and getting out in the fresh air more often, and is hydrating like crazy. She feels that she can't exactly tell others what to do if she isn't taking her own advice. Nice one, Aja: you do you!

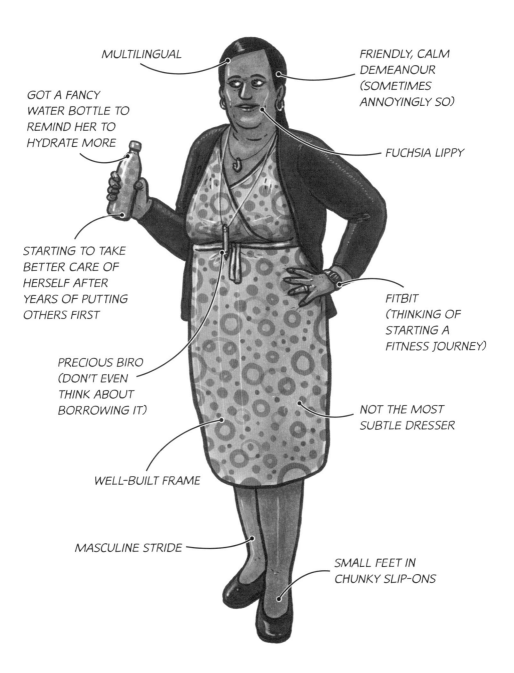

OLLIE THE LAD

Every group of friends needs an Ollie. It doesn't matter if it's a huge New Year's Eve event, a barbie and a game of backyard cricket or just a quick beer at the pub: you can always count on Ollie being there.

Ollie's a rare breed. He's one of those guys who transcends social groups. He gets on with nerds and jocks, girls and guys and everything in between. Ollie loves everyone and everyone loves Ollie.

After spending the last five years working in London and travelling through Europe, Ollie decided it was time to come home. He'd had an amazing time overseas, but he felt he was becoming a slave to the system—oh, and he also really missed his mum.

Ollie's loving life back in New Zealand: the summer weather has been great so far, the cricket's on, there's plenty of cold beer to go around, and his mum lives right around the corner. Enjoy the summer, Ollie!

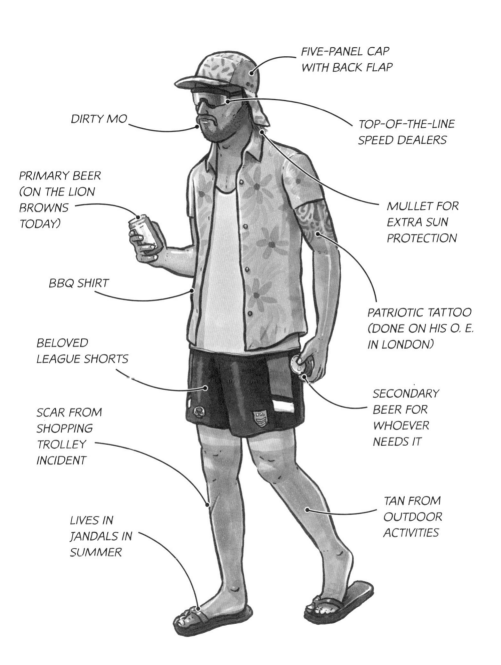

FIVE-PANEL CAP
WITH BACK FLAP

DIRTY MO

TOP-OF-THE-LINE
SPEED DEALERS

PRIMARY BEER
(ON THE LION
BROWNS
TODAY)

MULLET FOR
EXTRA SUN
PROTECTION

BBQ SHIRT

PATRIOTIC TATTOO
(DONE ON HIS O. E.
IN LONDON)

BELOVED
LEAGUE SHORTS

SECONDARY
BEER FOR
WHOEVER
NEEDS IT

SCAR FROM
SHOPPING
TROLLEY
INCIDENT

TAN FROM
OUTDOOR
ACTIVITIES

LIVES IN
JANDALS IN
SUMMER

ANXIOUS DAVO

Davo has had a pretty rough time in his 33 years on the planet. His upbringing wasn't the best and he's been mostly on his own since he was 15. That being said, Davo knows it's up to him to turn his life around and he'd better do it soon, as his missus has almost had enough of his antics. He's had a hard time leaving his younger days behind—hanging out with the boys, cruising around town in the car, getting up to all kinds of mischief.

Davo wants to be a better person, especially for his young daughters Kylie (two) and Kaitlyn (eight). He's applied for some factory work, as he knows that the busier he is, the less trouble he's likely to cause.

If he gets the job, the first thing Davo wants to do is start putting some money away for an overseas trip. He's always wanted to take the family over to Brisbane to see their gran. She's never met the kids and he knows that he'll be in the good books with his missus for ages if he can pull it off. Good luck, Davo!

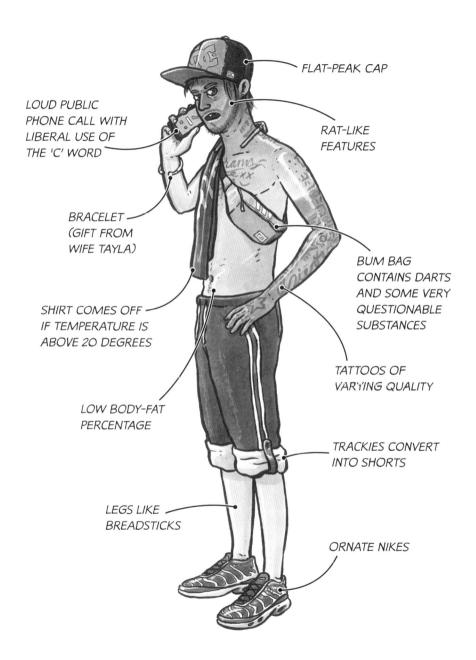

FLAT-PEAK CAP

LOUD PUBLIC PHONE CALL WITH LIBERAL USE OF THE 'C' WORD

RAT-LIKE FEATURES

BRACELET (GIFT FROM WIFE TAYLA)

BUM BAG CONTAINS DARTS AND SOME VERY QUESTIONABLE SUBSTANCES

SHIRT COMES OFF IF TEMPERATURE IS ABOVE 20 DEGREES

TATTOOS OF VARYING QUALITY

LOW BODY-FAT PERCENTAGE

TRACKIES CONVERT INTO SHORTS

LEGS LIKE BREADSTICKS

ORNATE NIKES

UPPER-MIDDLE-MANAGEMENT KERRI

Kerri has worked hard to get to where she is. She's lost count of the amount of networking she's done over the years and her LinkedIn account is growing stronger by the day. Although outwardly very confident, internally Kerri is always questioning her ability, and because her job is so intangible she's never really sure if she's doing it well or not.

Today, Kerri's diary is stacked. First up, she has a breakfast meeting with one of her media reps, then it's a quick turnaround for coffee with one of her suppliers. At 11 she's scheduled in a session with her personal trainer (she's heading to Hawai'i in May and wants to look her best), then after that she's heading to her favourite sushi place for lunch.

At 2 p.m. there's a senior leadership team meeting to discuss processes and workflow (it's catered so she'll get there early).

At about 4 p.m. she's added an offsite meeting into her diary, but she's actually just knocking off early to meet one of her girlfriends at a new wine bar in town. You go, Kerri! You only live once!

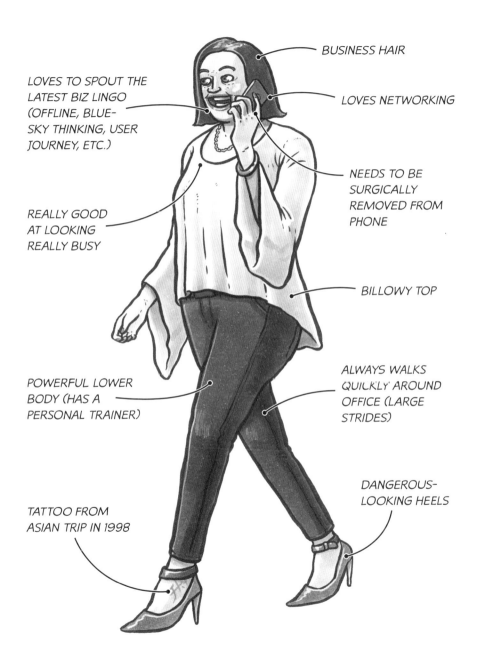

BUSINESS HAIR

LOVES TO SPOUT THE LATEST BIZ LINGO (OFFLINE, BLUE-SKY THINKING, USER JOURNEY, ETC.)

LOVES NETWORKING

NEEDS TO BE SURGICALLY REMOVED FROM PHONE

REALLY GOOD AT LOOKING REALLY BUSY

BILLOWY TOP

POWERFUL LOWER BODY (HAS A PERSONAL TRAINER)

ALWAYS WALKS QUICKLY AROUND OFFICE (LARGE STRIDES)

DANGEROUS-LOOKING HEELS

TATTOO FROM ASIAN TRIP IN 1998

PAINTING AND DECORATING CODY

Unlike most kids, Cody always knew what he wanted to do when he left school. He'd lined up his painting and decorating apprenticeship early, and couldn't wait to get out into the real world and start living life on his own terms.

His boss was a good guy, hard but fair. He made it pretty clear from the start that if Cody turned up early, worked hard and listened to what he was told, he'd do well.

Cody did all this and more. He worked hard and flew through his apprenticeship. These days Cody is a valued member of AAA Painting and Decorating, and even has a couple of young lads under him.

When not working, Cody loves working on his lowered and customised 2001 Mazda Bounty ute. You'll often see him bouncing down Maunganui Road at the Mount, eyeing up the local talent.

Although Cody loves working at AAA, he's been thinking of what his next move will be. Does he start his own business? Does he upgrade the ute? Should he go and check out Perth for a while? Whatever you do, Cody, you're bound to nail it!

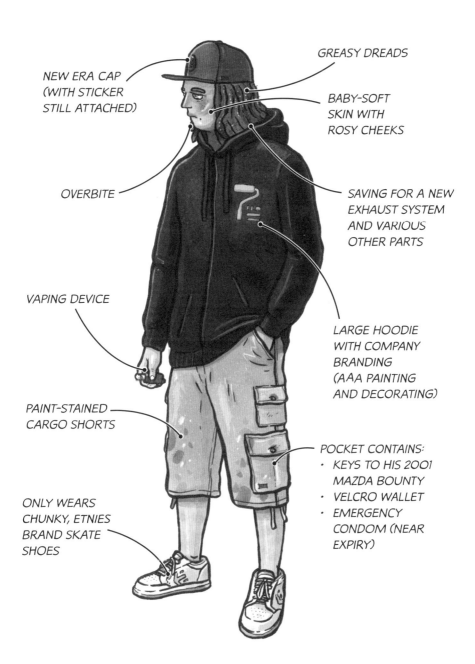

GREASY DREADS

NEW ERA CAP
(WITH STICKER
STILL ATTACHED)

BABY-SOFT
SKIN WITH
ROSY CHEEKS

OVERBITE

SAVING FOR A NEW
EXHAUST SYSTEM
AND VARIOUS
OTHER PARTS

VAPING DEVICE

LARGE HOODIE
WITH COMPANY
BRANDING
(AAA PAINTING
AND DECORATING)

PAINT-STAINED
CARGO SHORTS

POCKET CONTAINS:
· KEYS TO HIS 2001
MAZDA BOUNTY
· VELCRO WALLET
· EMERGENCY
CONDOM (NEAR
EXPIRY)

ONLY WEARS
CHUNKY, ETNIES
BRAND SKATE
SHOES

STYLE
PAGE
CASSIUS

He'll never admit to it, but the greatest day of Cassius's life was when he was stopped on the street by a photographer for a local fashion and lifestyle magazine. He'd always wanted to be featured in the city style pages. He absolutely revelled in talking about his bespoke brogues from Copenhagen, vintage Ray-Ban Clubmasters and super-high-thread-count shemagh from Cairo. When the kerbside interview was over, a sense of calm achievement washed over him: his dream had finally come true.

Later that night, Cassius woke suddenly. He had to get in the style pages again: true trendsetters get in multiple times. He grabbed his phone, logged on to a travel site and booked his flights to Europe.

Operation Style Icon had begun.

DREADING THE DAY WHEN FACIAL HAIR IS NO LONGER TRENDY

BEANIE FROM BERLIN

RAY-BAN CLUBMASTERS

DECORATIVE DOG TAGS

BEARD HIDES WEAK CHIN

$2500 BAG (AN INVESTMENT)

SMOKES ROLLIES FOR THAT BLUE-COLLAR EDGE

BAG CONTAINS:
· TWO LIGHTERS
· ONE MUESLI BAR
· ONE OVERDUE POWER BILL

CAREFULLY PERFECTED CATWALK-STYLE STRUT

EXTRA CLICKY SOLE

SHOES FROM COPENHAGEN

BAG LADY ROSSLYN

Rosslyn is a fixture at the local McDonald's café. She comes in about every second day and orders the same thing each time: a large cappuccino with three sugars and a cheese-and-onion toastie.

She sits in the same seat by the window each time, with her large shopping bag filled with junk mail placed beside her.

She sits quietly and methodically goes through her pile of papers, reading each page, circling products and muttering to herself, stopping only to say a quiet hello to anyone that might walk by. None of the staff really know why she does what she does, but she seems happy, and it'll be a sad day when she finally stops coming in.

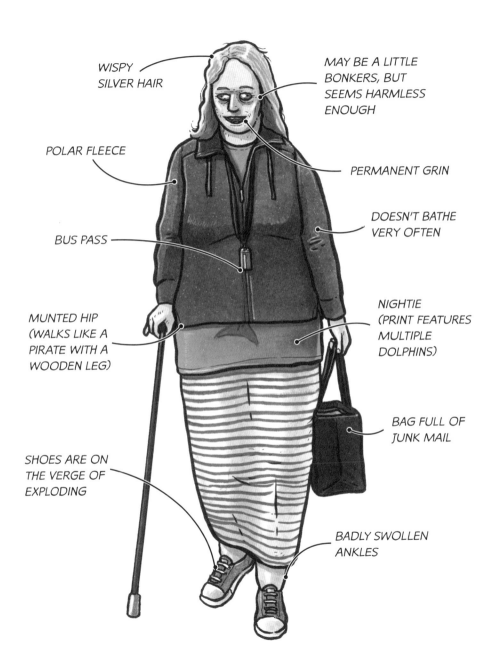

VERY
METAL
AIDEN

Aiden is very rarely seen without his headphones on. He says that his music is the only thing that stops him from strangling all the idiots on the bus to work every morning. During the day Aiden works as a web developer for a medium-sized creative agency. Although it's not the most challenging work, it's not too stressful either, and because the other departments don't really understand what a web developer does, they tend to leave him and the rest of his team alone.

When not working, Aiden loves to support the local metal scene; he's got some good mates in a few of the bands around town so he's never short of a gig to go to. He and his wife Anneke also enjoy playing the fantasy card game Magic: The Gathering, and they try to have a few of their friends over at least once a week for a long play session.

Next up for Aiden and Anneke is their long-overdue honeymoon. They're heading to Helsinki in Finland to see some of their favourite bands play the Tuska Open Air Metal Festival. Have a wild time, guys!

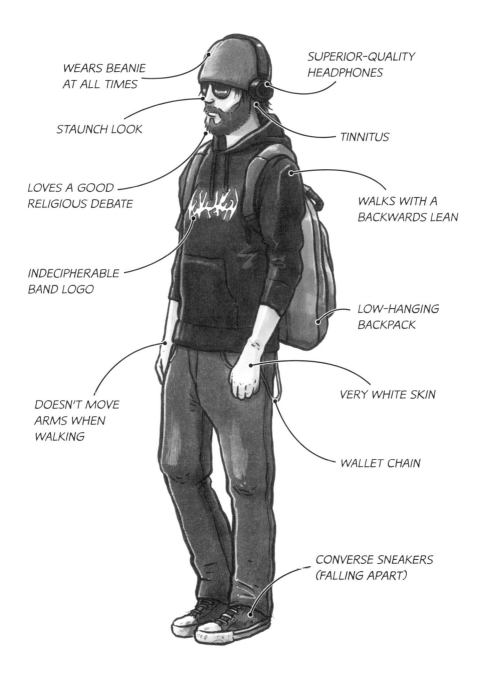

WEARS BEANIE
AT ALL TIMES

SUPERIOR-QUALITY
HEADPHONES

STAUNCH LOOK

TINNITUS

LOVES A GOOD
RELIGIOUS DEBATE

WALKS WITH A
BACKWARDS LEAN

INDECIPHERABLE
BAND LOGO

LOW-HANGING
BACKPACK

DOESN'T MOVE
ARMS WHEN
WALKING

VERY WHITE SKIN

WALLET CHAIN

CONVERSE SNEAKERS
(FALLING APART)

LOGISTICS COMPANY MATTY

Matty loves his family, his footy, his 2003 HSV Clubsport and putting in an honest day's work. But most of all, Matty loves early Friday afternoon knock-off. As soon as the clock hits four (earlier if it's quiet), Matty and the rest of the crew head off down the road to the local tavern. They've been going there for so long that Pat starts pouring the jugs as soon as they walk in. Matty pays for the first round of beers and gets a few fisherman's baskets to keep the boys from going too hard too soon.

Although a few of the lads will go home early, Matty and most of the guys will stick it out to the end, eventually gaining control of the jukebox and pool table.

Enjoy the rest of your evening, Matty! Remember to take the empties back up to the bar!

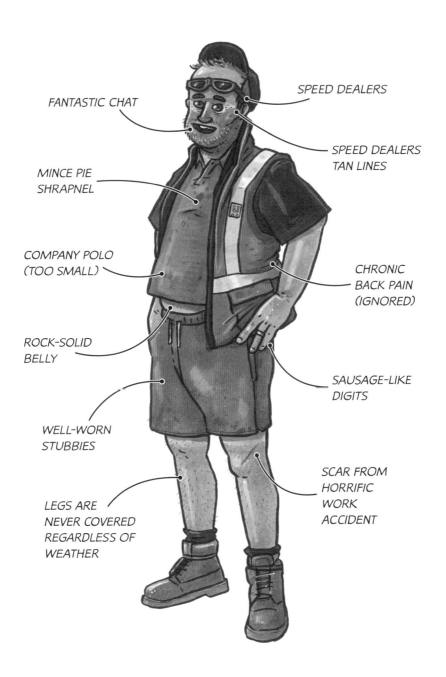

FANTASTIC CHAT

SPEED DEALERS

SPEED DEALERS
TAN LINES

MINCE PIE
SHRAPNEL

COMPANY POLO
(TOO SMALL)

CHRONIC
BACK PAIN
(IGNORED)

ROCK-SOLID
BELLY

SAUSAGE-LIKE
DIGITS

WELL-WORN
STUBBIES

LEGS ARE
NEVER COVERED
REGARDLESS OF
WEATHER

SCAR FROM
HORRIFIC
WORK
ACCIDENT

FESTIVAL BRIONY

Summer has arrived and Briony couldn't be happier. She's been planning her festival wardrobe for months, and now she finally gets to test out her purchases for real!

Briony has tickets to five festivals lined up already and she's just waiting to see who else is keen before committing to even more. She's memorised the line-up for all of them—she doesn't particularly like any of the music, but if someone asks about one of the bands she has to sound like she knows what she's talking about.

About a week out from the big day Briony begins selecting her event-specific outfit. She starts by browsing galleries from recent American and European festivals, taking notes on what the celebrity attendees are wearing. After the outfit selection comes the pose practice. You may think that all those coy, taken-off-guard photos come naturally, but no. Briony practises for hours in front of the mirror, sometimes even employing the services of her hapless boyfriend as photographer to perfect the look. Enjoy festival season, Briony!

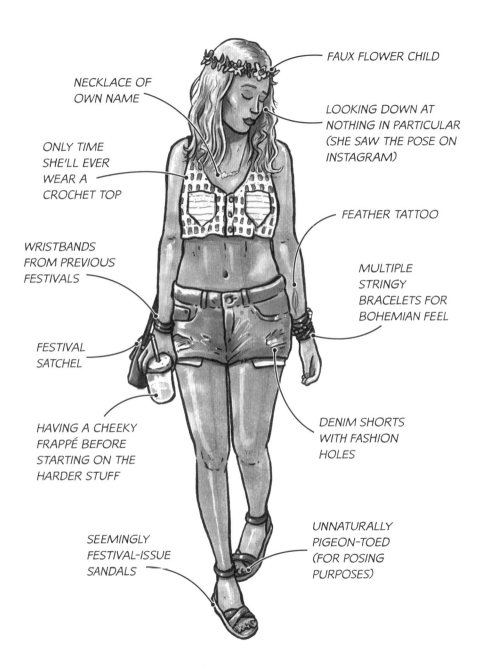

FAUX FLOWER CHILD

NECKLACE OF OWN NAME

LOOKING DOWN AT NOTHING IN PARTICULAR (SHE SAW THE POSE ON INSTAGRAM)

ONLY TIME SHE'LL EVER WEAR A CROCHET TOP

FEATHER TATTOO

WRISTBANDS FROM PREVIOUS FESTIVALS

MULTIPLE STRINGY BRACELETS FOR BOHEMIAN FEEL

FESTIVAL SATCHEL

HAVING A CHEEKY FRAPPÉ BEFORE STARTING ON THE HARDER STUFF

DENIM SHORTS WITH FASHION HOLES

UNNATURALLY PIGEON-TOED (FOR POSING PURPOSES)

SEEMINGLY FESTIVAL-ISSUE SANDALS

WEDDING KANE

Nobody ruins a carefully prepared wedding photo like Kane. Completely ignoring the dress code, Kane's dusted off the old three-piece that he last wore at the Addington races in 2008. He's teamed it up with his best high-top sneakers and ever-present Dirty Dog sunnies.

He may not look the part, but you can't leave old Kano off the guest list. He mixes well with everyone and he'll keep some of the older guests entertained with his great yarns. For most people, listening to stories about lawn edging or the difficulties in clearing out guttering would be an absolute bore, but Kane always seems so genuinely interested in what people have to say.

You know Kane will stick around until the end, help clean up the venue and make sure the old loves get to their taxis. He may be scruffy, but he's an absolute legend!

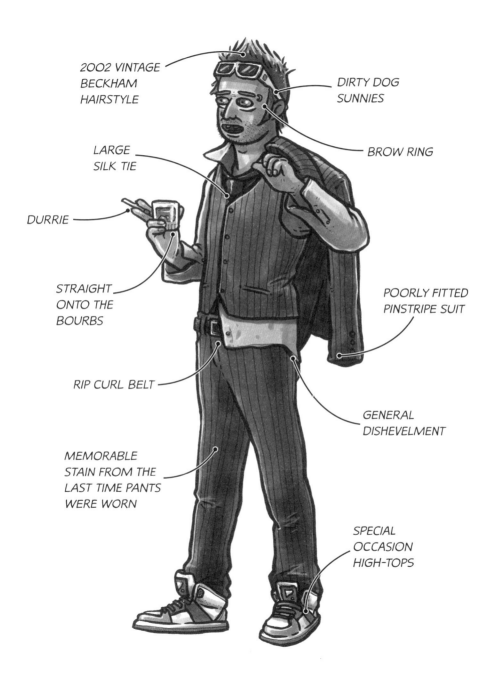

2002 VINTAGE BECKHAM HAIRSTYLE

DIRTY DOG SUNNIES

BROW RING

LARGE SILK TIE

DURRIE

STRAIGHT ONTO THE BOURBS

POORLY FITTED PINSTRIPE SUIT

RIP CURL BELT

GENERAL DISHEVELMENT

MEMORABLE STAIN FROM THE LAST TIME PANTS WERE WORN

SPECIAL OCCASION HIGH-TOPS

BIG JESSE

Big Jesse easily has the strength and skill to destroy you, but luckily for us, he uses his immense power for good, not evil.

With his physical size and sporting prowess, Jesse could easily have been the typical cocky jock at school, but his mum raised him well and he's turned into a good, respectful young man.

During the week, Jesse works at the headquarters of a big telco in Auckland. His work ethic and personable nature have impressed everyone he's worked with, and management have said that if he keeps it up he can go places within the organisation.

When not working or helping out the family, Jesse loves spending time with his mates, usually cruising around town in his Blue Mica 2003 Subaru WRX wagon with custom wheels and exhaust.

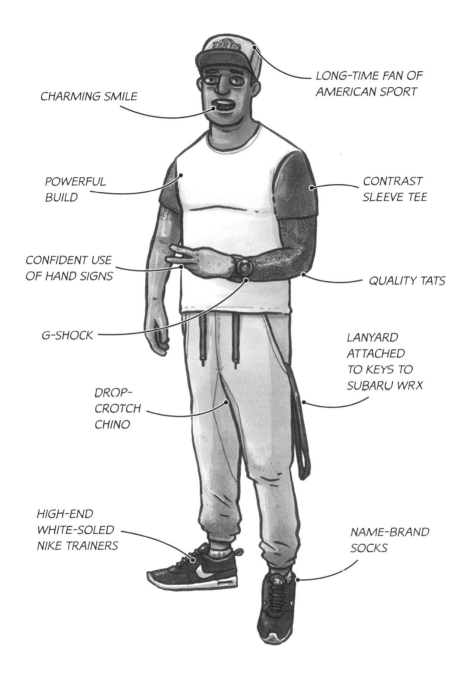

CHARMING SMILE

LONG-TIME FAN OF AMERICAN SPORT

POWERFUL BUILD

CONTRAST SLEEVE TEE

CONFIDENT USE OF HAND SIGNS

QUALITY TATS

G-SHOCK

LANYARD ATTACHED TO KEYS TO SUBARU WRX

DROP-CROTCH CHINO

HIGH-END WHITE-SOLED NIKE TRAINERS

NAME-BRAND SOCKS

TOUR GROUP GRACE

Grace's eldest son Michael had studied in New Zealand and loved it. Although the pace of life was slower than in Seoul, he loved the fact that, if you wanted to, you could swim at a beach in the morning, climb a mountain at lunchtime and be back in the city for a drink at the pub before it got dark. Everything seemed so accessible.

Grace had seen all of his amazing photos and couldn't wait to visit. She and a few of her friends decided that a tour group was the best way to go. They hadn't really travelled much and weren't too confident about driving, as they'd heard some horror stories.

So far the trip has been amazing, but there's one part she's looking forward to more than anything: Michael is going to meet her in Queenstown. He's taken some time off from his job in Los Angeles so he can show her some of his favourite places. Have an awesome time, Grace, and don't forget to buy some possum-fur slippers!

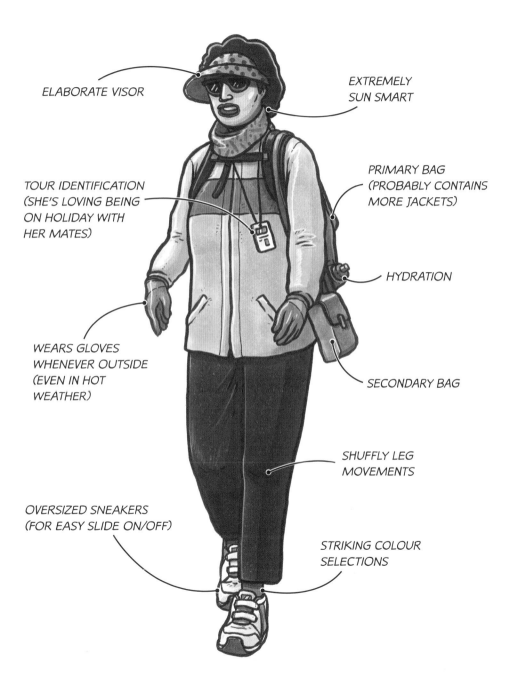

ELABORATE VISOR

EXTREMELY
SUN SMART

TOUR IDENTIFICATION
(SHE'S LOVING BEING
ON HOLIDAY WITH
HER MATES)

PRIMARY BAG
(PROBABLY CONTAINS
MORE JACKETS)

HYDRATION

WEARS GLOVES
WHENEVER OUTSIDE
(EVEN IN HOT
WEATHER)

SECONDARY BAG

SHUFFLY LEG
MOVEMENTS

OVERSIZED SNEAKERS
(FOR EASY SLIDE ON/OFF)

STRIKING COLOUR
SELECTIONS

BACKYARD SCOTTY

Parties at Scotty's place are usually pretty solid. He's invited Aaron, Scooter and Dazza around early so they can have some guy time before the girls arrive. Usually they start off by parking their heavily modified Rotaries nose to nose so they can yarn and compare notes as they noisily idle.

As the day progresses, the duty-free bourbon (from a recent trip to Oz) flows and the Salmonella Dub gets louder.

Night falls and things get a little more rowdy; Aaron has already passed out on the picnic table, and it's just a matter of time until Scotty breaks out the old BMX to perform a few stunts.

Just another classic do at Scotty's place.

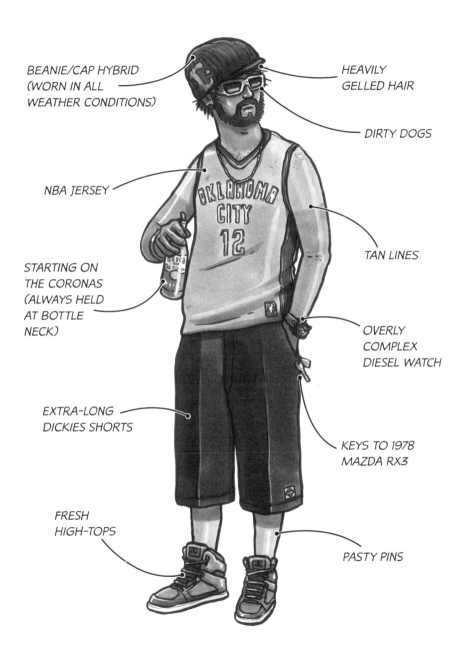

BEANIE/CAP HYBRID (WORN IN ALL WEATHER CONDITIONS)

HEAVILY GELLED HAIR

DIRTY DOGS

NBA JERSEY

TAN LINES

STARTING ON THE CORONAS (ALWAYS HELD AT BOTTLE NECK)

OVERLY COMPLEX DIESEL WATCH

EXTRA-LONG DICKIES SHORTS

KEYS TO 1978 MAZDA RX3

FRESH HIGH-TOPS

PASTY PINS

WEEKEND WARRIOR JOSEPH

He's lost a bit of speed over the years, and the body might take a little longer to recover, but that doesn't stop 41-year-old Joseph from schooling a few of the younger lads in second grade.

Back in the day Joseph was an impressive player, and he knows that, with a little more application and better luck with injuries, he could have made a career of it—but right now, at this moment, he has no regrets.

These days for Joseph it's more about blowing out the cobwebs from a work week stuck behind a desk than trying to knock over the opposition. He may feel knackered after a full 80 minutes of tough league, but there's nothing better than having a few cold ones with his mates after another hard-fought loss.

Good on ya, Joseph: enjoy that post-match nutrition.

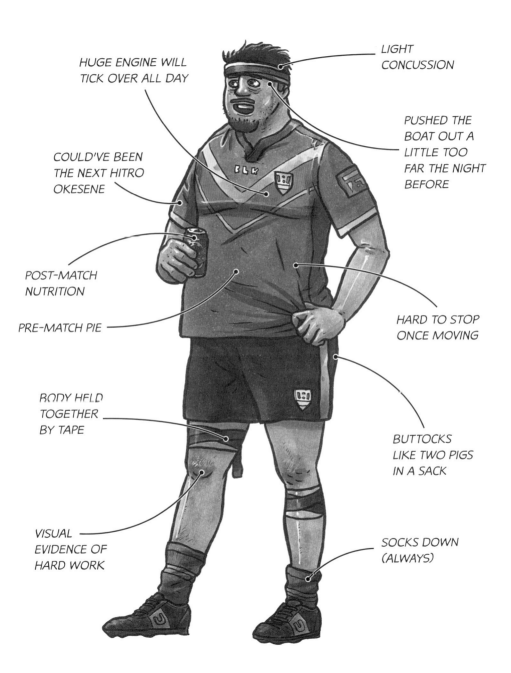

HUGE ENGINE WILL TICK OVER ALL DAY

LIGHT CONCUSSION

PUSHED THE BOAT OUT A LITTLE TOO FAR THE NIGHT BEFORE

COULD'VE BEEN THE NEXT HITRO OKESENE

POST-MATCH NUTRITION

PRE-MATCH PIE

HARD TO STOP ONCE MOVING

BODY HELD TOGETHER BY TAPE

BUTTOCKS LIKE TWO PIGS IN A SACK

VISUAL EVIDENCE OF HARD WORK

SOCKS DOWN (ALWAYS)

SELF-CHECKOUT AMY

Amy's been working at the supermarket for almost eight years now, and although it's not exactly the most glamorous job in the world, the place has been really good to her, and the flexible hours and understanding management have made raising her two kids a lot easier.

For the past few months Amy has been the overlord of the self-checkout section of the supermarket. Her main tasks are to keep traffic moving smoothly through the area and make sure that customers pay for everything in their bags. She doesn't really care if you say your SweeTango apples are the cheaper Royal Galas; just don't try and pass off an avocado as an unwashed potato, because if you do there's going to be trouble. Sock it to 'em, Amy!

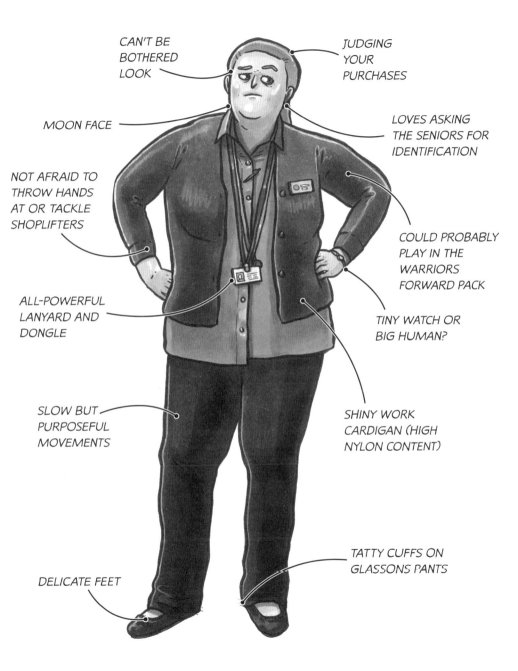

CAN'T BE BOTHERED LOOK

JUDGING YOUR PURCHASES

MOON FACE

LOVES ASKING THE SENIORS FOR IDENTIFICATION

NOT AFRAID TO THROW HANDS AT OR TACKLE SHOPLIFTERS

COULD PROBABLY PLAY IN THE WARRIORS FORWARD PACK

ALL-POWERFUL LANYARD AND DONGLE

TINY WATCH OR BIG HUMAN?

SLOW BUT PURPOSEFUL MOVEMENTS

SHINY WORK CARDIGAN (HIGH NYLON CONTENT)

DELICATE FEET

TATTY CUFFS ON GLASSONS PANTS

NIGHT
OUT
BLAKE

The crew at the local sign shop have been working super hard lately, and it's been far too long since they all got together and let off a bit of steam. The girls and guys at the shop are a great bunch, so to show his appreciation Blake's decided to book a table at the local Lone Star restaurant and shout them all dinner and drinks.

Blake started at the sign shop straight after he finished high school and has moved his way from shop hand to machine operator, then through the design department and all the way up to manager.

Blake loves the variety of work he gets to do each day. Earlier in the week he was putting up signage in a supermarket, yesterday he was learning how to use a new vinyl-cutting machine, and next month he's off to the New Zealand Sign and Display Awards. But none of that would be any fun without a great team.

Enjoy your big evening, Blake: your crew love ya to bits.

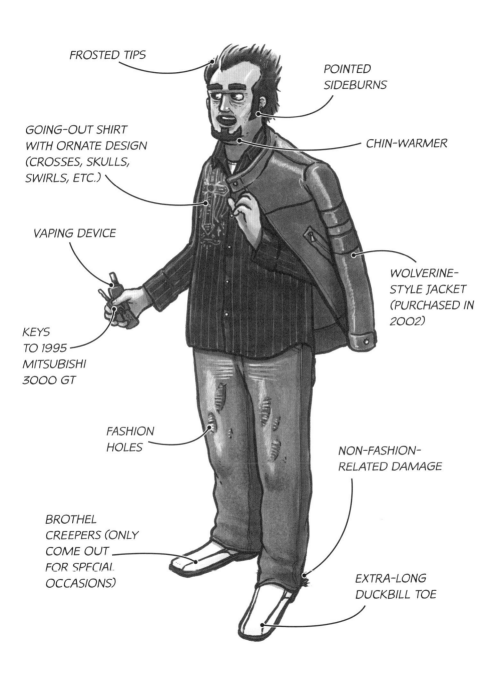

FROSTED TIPS

POINTED SIDEBURNS

GOING-OUT SHIRT WITH ORNATE DESIGN (CROSSES, SKULLS, SWIRLS, ETC.)

CHIN-WARMER

VAPING DEVICE

WOLVERINE-STYLE JACKET (PURCHASED IN 2002)

KEYS TO 1995 MITSUBISHI 3000 GT

FASHION HOLES

NON-FASHION-RELATED DAMAGE

BROTHEL CREEPERS (ONLY COME OUT FOR SPECIAL OCCASIONS)

EXTRA-LONG DUCKBILL TOE

SUNDAY
SESH
DES

Des has had a pretty busy Sunday. He's mowed the lawns, cleared out the guttering, taken a load of garden waste to the dump and even visited his sister-in-law. There's no way his wife can stop him from going to the pub now!

If you're heading down to the local this Sunday afternoon for a quiet drink, make sure you don't make too much eye contact with Des. Otherwise, he'll be over in a flash to tell you his life story. Again.

He's now a few beers deep into his session, and really warming to his work. He's currently talking to the customer next to him (the customer has no idea he's being talked to) about what a bad idea the capital gains tax was and how it's all the fault of lazy young people.

After a few more brews, Des becomes an even bigger pest and enjoys having a cheeky flirt with the younger bar girls. He's convinced that they love his yarns and can't resist the old Des magic.

Late in the evening, after being denied a drink for the second time, Des makes the wobbly trek home, flops into his favourite chair and falls asleep. Rest easy, Des.

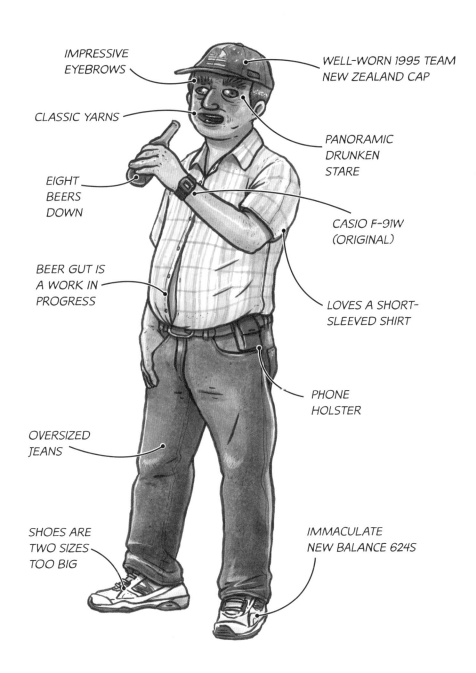

IMPRESSIVE EYEBROWS

WELL-WORN 1995 TEAM NEW ZEALAND CAP

CLASSIC YARNS

PANORAMIC DRUNKEN STARE

EIGHT BEERS DOWN

CASIO F-91W (ORIGINAL)

BEER GUT IS A WORK IN PROGRESS

LOVES A SHORT-SLEEVED SHIRT

OVERSIZED JEANS

PHONE HOLSTER

SHOES ARE TWO SIZES TOO BIG

IMMACULATE NEW BALANCE 624S

QUIRKY BEATRIX

Beatrix will freely admit that she wasn't the most interesting person in high school. She studied hard and got good grades, but she felt she didn't make the most of the social side of her time.

That all changed when she moved from her home town of Oamaru to Wellington to go to university. Gone were the stuffy uniforms and rules of school: away from her family and old school friends, she was free to reinvent herself.

She started going to gigs, buying second-hand clothing and spending countless hours in inner-city cafés, updating her Tumblr account and listening to podcasts about serial killers. She feels she's finally beginning to feel comfortable in her own skin.

Although Beatrix (or 'B', as her uni friends call her) loves her new life in Wellington, Oamaru will always have her heart. She's heading back there next month for her dad's fiftieth birthday and she can't wait to impress everyone with her exciting tales of life in the big city.

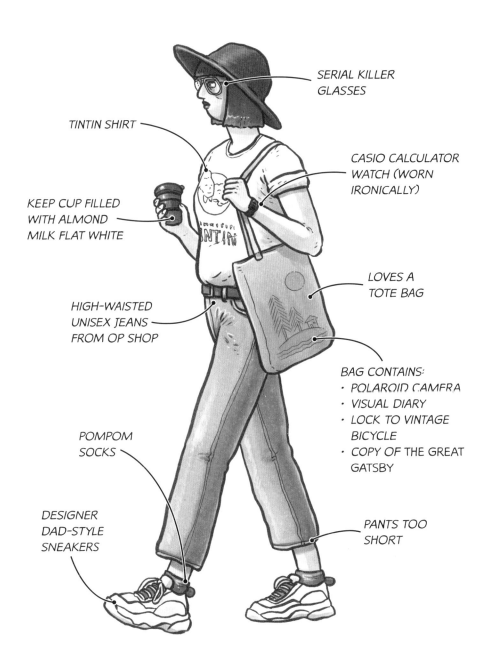

SERIAL KILLER GLASSES

TINTIN SHIRT

CASIO CALCULATOR WATCH (WORN IRONICALLY)

KEEP CUP FILLED WITH ALMOND MILK FLAT WHITE

LOVES A TOTE BAG

HIGH-WAISTED UNISEX JEANS FROM OP SHOP

BAG CONTAINS:
· POLAROID CAMERA
· VISUAL DIARY
· LOCK TO VINTAGE BICYCLE
· COPY OF THE GREAT GATSBY

POMPOM SOCKS

DESIGNER DAD-STYLE SNEAKERS

PANTS TOO SHORT

LUNCHING PRUE

Nobody brunches and lunches quite like Prue, who can turn a standard casual catch-up into an all-day, wine-fuelled affair.

Today she's meeting up with fellow pro-lunchers Bethany and Eleanor for their usual early-afternoon Wednesday session. She loves these little rendezvous, as they give her the chance to unload all the stresses of the week. Issues for discussion today include: the amount of golf her husband Grant's been playing, Sandra's new hairstyle (what was she thinking?), whether or not to sell the boutique, and planning activities for the midwinter trip to Bora Bora.

Good luck, Prue! Hope you sort everything out!

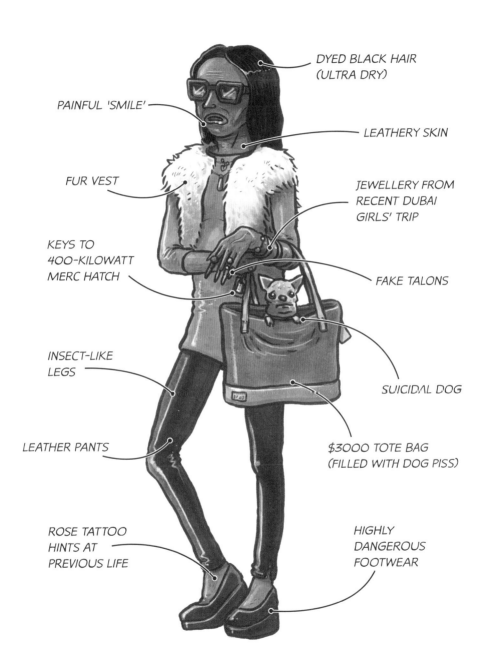

DYED BLACK HAIR
(ULTRA DRY)

PAINFUL 'SMILE'

LEATHERY SKIN

FUR VEST

JEWELLERY FROM
RECENT DUBAI
GIRLS' TRIP

KEYS TO
400-KILOWATT
MERC HATCH

FAKE TALONS

INSECT-LIKE
LEGS

SUICIDAL DOG

LEATHER PANTS

$3000 TOTE BAG
(FILLED WITH DOG PISS)

ROSE TATTOO
HINTS AT
PREVIOUS LIFE

HIGHLY
DANGEROUS
FOOTWEAR

FAST-WALKING ANDY

Andy can usually be seen head down, hands in pockets, power-walking through the central city. Andy always looks like he has somewhere he needs to be, and that's the problem for Andy: he doesn't really need to be anywhere.

Andy spends his mornings surfing the internet at the local library. He usually starts by watching a few music videos, then moves on to heavier stuff involving government conspiracies and flat Earth theories.

When he's done at the library, Andy heads down to the local TAB to see his mates. In between pints, he rummages through the betting-slips bin: with any luck he'll find a few pints' worth of accidentally discarded winners. Fingers crossed, Andy!

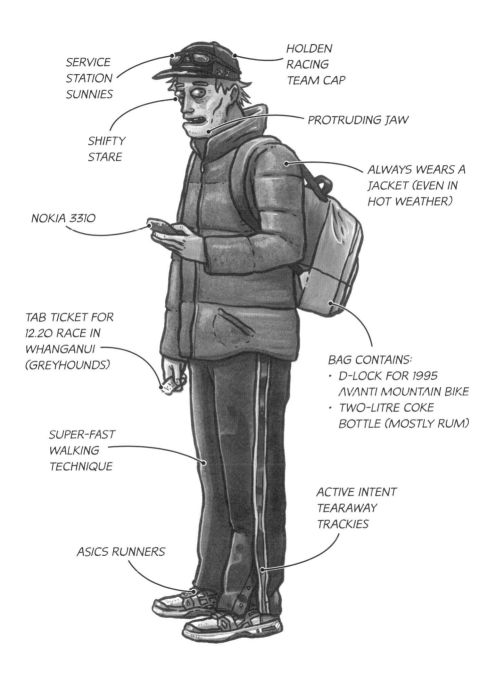

SERVICE STATION SUNNIES

HOLDEN RACING TEAM CAP

SHIFTY STARE

PROTRUDING JAW

ALWAYS WEARS A JACKET (EVEN IN HOT WEATHER)

NOKIA 3310

TAB TICKET FOR 12.20 RACE IN WHANGANUI (GREYHOUNDS)

BAG CONTAINS:
· D-LOCK FOR 1995 AVANTI MOUNTAIN BIKE
· TWO-LITRE COKE BOTTLE (MOSTLY RUM)

SUPER-FAST WALKING TECHNIQUE

ACTIVE INTENT TEARAWAY TRACKIES

ASICS RUNNERS

EIGHT-WEEK CHALLENGE KAT

Kat had an interesting time of it last year. She's the first to admit that she didn't take her relationship break-up well, but she's a lot better now and feels that going through that emotional hardship has made her a better, stronger person.

Kat is determined to make the most of this year. She's focusing on herself for the first time in ages and is feeling more alive than ever. Work is going well, her meal prep is on point and she's finally begun her fitness journey. Last year she completed the Queenstown 5K run and hopes to step up to the half marathon this time.

In a couple of months she's heading to Thailand for a girls' trip with her bestie Bec, so they're both working hard on their beach bodies.

Reach those goals, Kat, and live your best life!

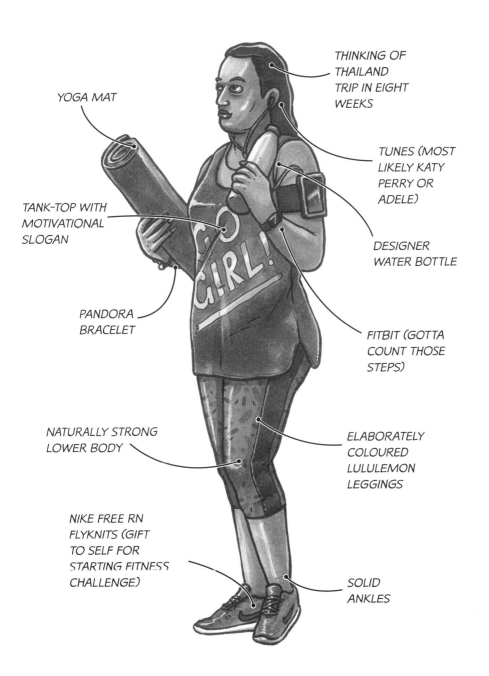

YOGA MAT

THINKING OF THAILAND TRIP IN EIGHT WEEKS

TUNES (MOST LIKELY KATY PERRY OR ADELE)

TANK-TOP WITH MOTIVATIONAL SLOGAN

DESIGNER WATER BOTTLE

PANDORA BRACELET

FITBIT (GOTTA COUNT THOSE STEPS)

NATURALLY STRONG LOWER BODY

ELABORATELY COLOURED LULULEMON LEGGINGS

NIKE FREE RN FLYKNITS (GIFT TO SELF FOR STARTING FITNESS CHALLENGE)

SOLID ANKLES

6.30 A.M.
FLIGHT TO
SYDNEY
TASHA

It's 4.30 a.m., and it's already been a long day for Tasha. She finished packing at about 4.10 a.m. and only just remembered her passport because she'd left it in her bag last time she went overseas. She's currently waiting in line at the ticketing counter, staring into space, oblivious to the ground crew waving her forward.

She may look like a dribbling, tracksuited zombie now, but see her in about 12 hours and you'd swear she was a different person. Tasha and her girlfriends have been planning this weekend in Sydney for months, and their clubbing outfits have been locked in for weeks.

Although her flight is only three and a half hours long, Tasha's carry-on baggage is close to bursting; it looks like she has enough equipment for a return mission to Alpha Centauri.

Good luck getting those bags through as carry-on luggage!

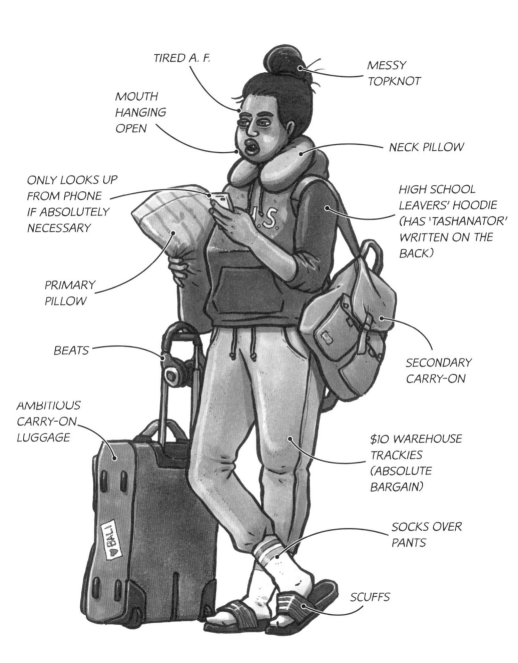

TIRED A. F.

MESSY
TOPKNOT

MOUTH
HANGING
OPEN

NECK PILLOW

ONLY LOOKS UP
FROM PHONE
IF ABSOLUTELY
NECESSARY

HIGH SCHOOL
LEAVERS' HOODIE
(HAS 'TASHANATOR'
WRITTEN ON THE
BACK)

PRIMARY
PILLOW

BEATS

SECONDARY
CARRY-ON

AMBITIOUS
CARRY-ON
LUGGAGE

$10 WAREHOUSE
TRACKIES
(ABSOLUTE
BARGAIN)

SOCKS OVER
PANTS

SCUFFS

BALI

HILUX
SURF
DREW

It's early Saturday morning, and Drew's just picked up a couple of Bacon and Egg McMuffins for breakfast. He may be feeling a little dusty from the night before, but that won't stop him fulfilling his weekend commitments. After he's smashed breakfast, he'll jump into his '89 Hilux Surf and head out to South Canterbury.

He's meeting up with a few friends at a spot near the Rakaia River for a day's hunting, and if all goes well they might get a few pigs, goats or deer. His mate Ricky's having his twenty-first birthday out there later, too, so if he kicks on, he'll probably sleep in the truck tonight.

Don't drink and drive, Drew.

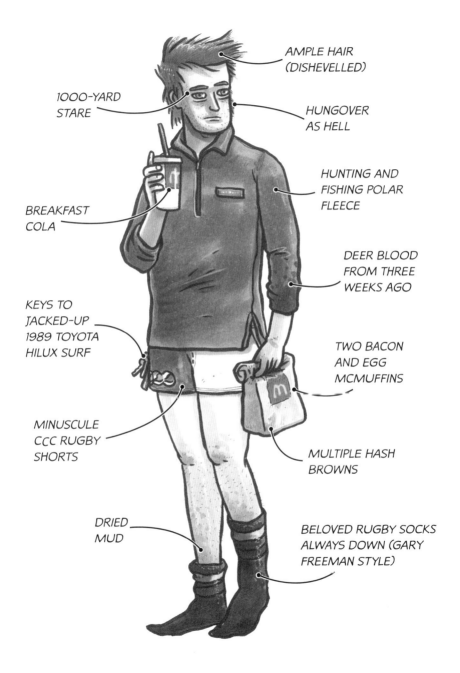

AMPLE HAIR
(DISHEVELLED)

1000-YARD
STARE

HUNGOVER
AS HELL

HUNTING AND
FISHING POLAR
FLEECE

BREAKFAST
COLA

DEER BLOOD
FROM THREE
WEEKS AGO

KEYS TO
JACKED-UP
1989 TOYOTA
HILUX SURF

TWO BACON
AND EGG
MCMUFFINS

MINUSCULE
CCC RUGBY
SHORTS

MULTIPLE HASH
BROWNS

DRIED
MUD

BELOVED RUGBY SOCKS
ALWAYS DOWN (GARY
FREEMAN STYLE)

HELPFUL BERYL

It doesn't matter whether she's your gran, mum, auntie or friend, everyone should treasure the Beryl in their lives. Beryl's children may have moved away, and her husband may have passed many years ago, but that doesn't mean she doesn't lead a busy and productive life.

She fills her days doing what Beryls do best: being helpful. Beryl has several events lined up for the next month, including three school bake sales, a fundraiser for the community pool and her regular gig organising the weekly bridge-club evening.

Beryls are easily spotted in the wild: look out for their familiar uniform of silver hair, comfortable shoes and red sleeveless polar fleece. If you see one, be sure to say hi: if you're lucky, she might invite you over for her legendary shepherd's pie and a cup of tea.

Bless you, Beryl.

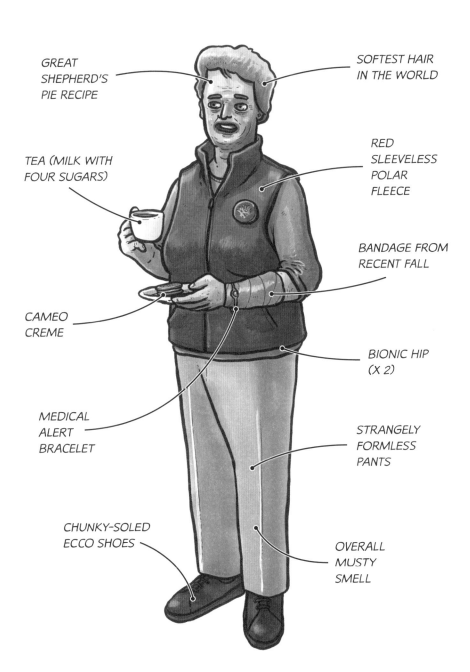

GREAT SHEPHERD'S PIE RECIPE

SOFTEST HAIR IN THE WORLD

TEA (MILK WITH FOUR SUGARS)

RED SLEEVELESS POLAR FLEECE

BANDAGE FROM RECENT FALL

CAMEO CREME

BIONIC HIP (X 2)

MEDICAL ALERT BRACELET

STRANGELY FORMLESS PANTS

CHUNKY-SOLED ECCO SHOES

OVERALL MUSTY SMELL

OFFICE JAN

Screw the work she was hired for: Jan has far more important things to do. She's currently organising a morning tea to raise money for the construction of a local swimming pool. Jan's spent a fair amount of time sourcing the perfect bunting to decorate the kitchen, and if everything goes well, they'll make enough cash to offset the expenses she rang up for the event.

Every office should have a Jan; they really are indispensable in a modern work environment. Are you the new guy? Jan will show you around. Can't find the leave forms? Jan will sort you out. Running out of sav during Friday-night drinks? Jan will reveal the secret stash.

When not bustling about the office or gossiping away in the kitchen, Jan can be seen powering around the block with her lunchtime walking group. Get that step count up, Jan!

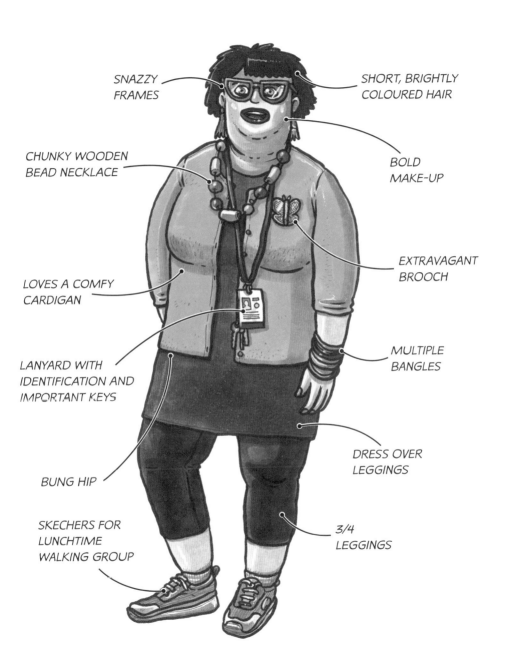

SNAZZY FRAMES

SHORT, BRIGHTLY COLOURED HAIR

CHUNKY WOODEN BEAD NECKLACE

BOLD MAKE-UP

EXTRAVAGANT BROOCH

LOVES A COMFY CARDIGAN

MULTIPLE BANGLES

LANYARD WITH IDENTIFICATION AND IMPORTANT KEYS

DRESS OVER LEGGINGS

BUNG HIP

3/4 LEGGINGS

SKECHERS FOR LUNCHTIME WALKING GROUP

UNCLE
PAULIE

Paulie always seems to have something on the go. Today he's popped into the pub on his way to check out a used car he saw on Trade Me.

Apparently the guy wants $900 for the Daihatsu Charade, but Paulie reckons he can get him down to $600. Paulie's been looking for a new ride ever since his cousin wrote off his old Laser, and he's getting sick of riding around on his old 10-speed pushbike. If he can get the Charade for a good price, he'll bring back some of the cash he's saved for a few beers and a solid hoon on the pokies. Good luck with the car, Paulie!

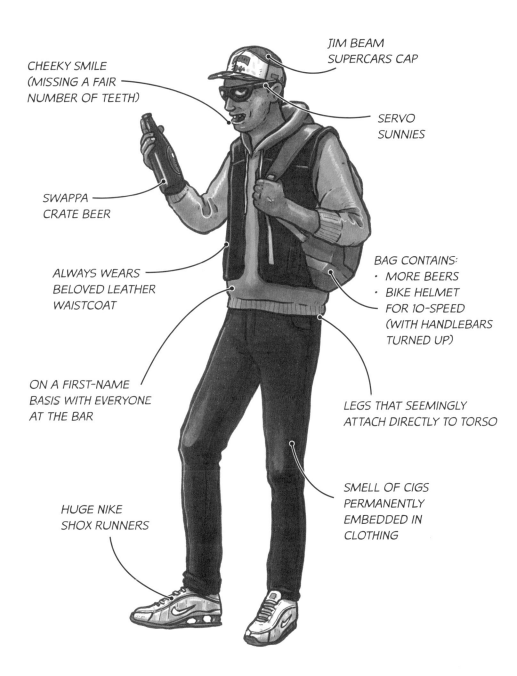

JIM BEAM SUPERCARS CAP

CHEEKY SMILE (MISSING A FAIR NUMBER OF TEETH)

SERVO SUNNIES

SWAPPA CRATE BEER

BAG CONTAINS:
· MORE BEERS
· BIKE HELMET FOR 10-SPEED (WITH HANDLEBARS TURNED UP)

ALWAYS WEARS BELOVED LEATHER WAISTCOAT

ON A FIRST-NAME BASIS WITH EVERYONE AT THE BAR

LEGS THAT SEEMINGLY ATTACH DIRECTLY TO TORSO

HUGE NIKE SHOX RUNNERS

SMELL OF CIGS PERMANENTLY EMBEDDED IN CLOTHING

SUNDAY MALL CRYSTAL

Crystal had a pretty big night last night, but she's managed to drag herself down to the mall to find a hangover cure. She's definitely going to have a diet Coke, but can't decide if she wants Macca's or a giant plate of sweet and sour pork. Maybe she'll get the Macca's now and take the sweet and sour pork home for later.

Her mum made her bring her little brother, so after her feed, she'll probably drop him off at The Warehouse to play on the PlayStations; that'll give her some time to shuffle down to Glassons for a browse in peace.

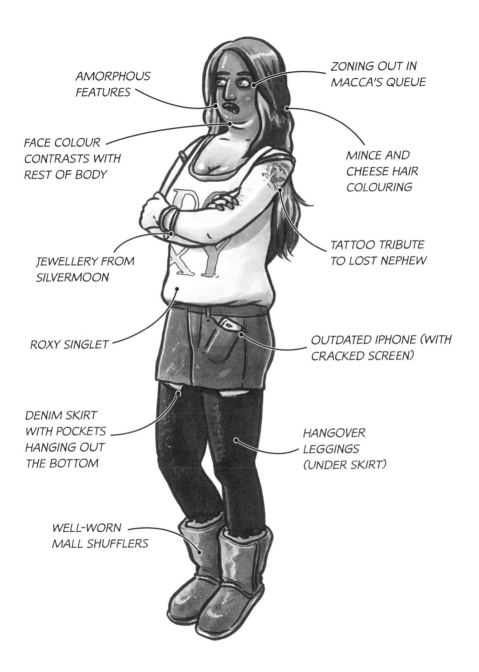

AMORPHOUS
FEATURES

ZONING OUT IN
MACCA'S QUEUE

FACE COLOUR
CONTRASTS WITH
REST OF BODY

MINCE AND
CHEESE HAIR
COLOURING

TATTOO TRIBUTE
TO LOST NEPHEW

JEWELLERY FROM
SILVERMOON

ROXY SINGLET

OUTDATED IPHONE (WITH
CRACKED SCREEN)

DENIM SKIRT
WITH POCKETS
HANGING OUT
THE BOTTOM

HANGOVER
LEGGINGS
(UNDER SKIRT)

WELL-WORN
MALL SHUFFLERS

BEASTLY BETH

Beth has just finished up her weekly shop at Pak'nSave and, by the looks of it, it didn't go smoothly. As usual, her children Blaze and Chastity used the supermarket as their own personal playground, and no amount of yelling and swearing from Beth could stop them.

She's managed to bribe the two rascals into the back of the AU Falcon with the promise of KFC so, hopefully, the ride home will be a little more peaceful.

Beth can usually be seen looking around from the front seat of her car, swearing loudly at the noisy kids. Although her sturdy frame and brooding presence scream violence and aggression, Beth does have a softer side. She loves bright colours, butterflies (she has seven butterfly tattoos of varying quality) and Ronan Keating. Don't let that lull you into a false sense of security though; she will f*ck you up good if you look at her the wrong way.

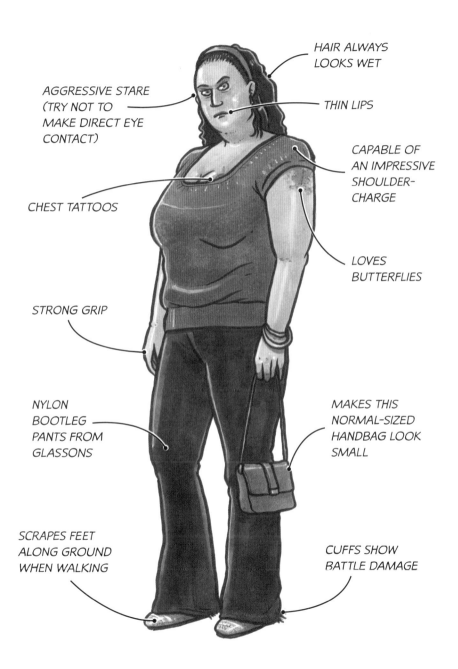

HAIR ALWAYS LOOKS WET

THIN LIPS

AGGRESSIVE STARE (TRY NOT TO MAKE DIRECT EYE CONTACT)

CAPABLE OF AN IMPRESSIVE SHOULDER-CHARGE

CHEST TATTOOS

LOVES BUTTERFLIES

STRONG GRIP

NYLON BOOTLEG PANTS FROM GLASSONS

MAKES THIS NORMAL-SIZED HANDBAG LOOK SMALL

SCRAPES FEET ALONG GROUND WHEN WALKING

CUFFS SHOW BATTLE DAMAGE

FRIDAY MORNING RORY

Rory knows he shouldn't have gone so hard last night, but sometimes when the weather's right and the lads are on form, he can't help himself. Rory's stopped off at the service station to grab his usual breakfast of an energy drink and a bacon and egg pie. His semi-nutritious meal should set him up well for a busy day on the building site.

Although Rory's no stranger to a hard day's yakka, he's hoping that the lunchtime rain that's forecast does eventuate, so that he and the boys can finish early and get back on the cans. Pace yourself, Rory!

HUNGOVER BUT STILL CHEERFUL

AERIAL SERVO SUNNIES

MULLET

BREAKFAST OF CHAMPIONS (BACON AND EGG PIE)

DUNNIE BLUES

HUGE ENERGY DRINK SHOULD TAKE THE EDGE OFF

TRIBAL TATTOO

LONG-SERVING FLANNEL SHIRT

ROCK LOGO TEE

LYNX AFRICA FOR SHOWER ON THE GO (SLEPT IN SO DIDN'T HAVE TIME TO MAKE HIMSELF LOOK PRETTY)

RUGBY SOCKS

REDBACK SAFETY BOOTS

HIKING FRANK

It's been almost three years since Frank's wife Edith passed away, and although he still misses her dearly, he takes comfort in knowing that she's no longer in pain. Edith's passing made Frank re-evaluate his life. Gone are the lazy mornings in bed and the wasted afternoons in front of the television; in their place are sunrise hikes and laughter-filled coffee (sometimes beer) dates with neglected friends. Frank loves getting out in the fresh air now. He tries to do a new hike each week and has vowed to see as much of the beautiful New Zealand countryside as his dodgy knees will allow. He just wishes Edith were here to enjoy it all with him.

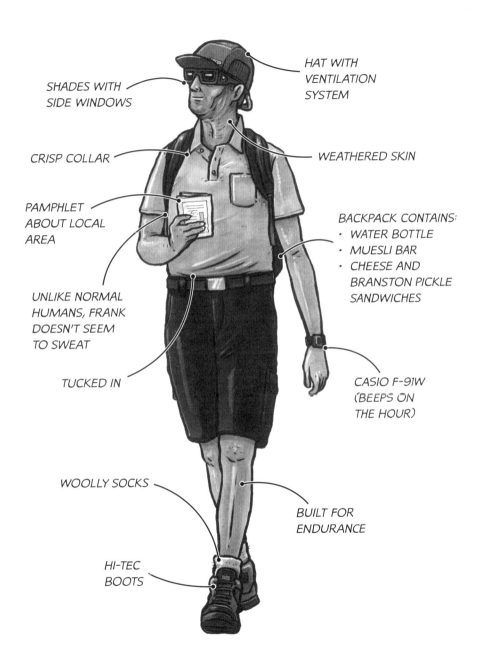

HAT WITH
VENTILATION
SYSTEM

SHADES WITH
SIDE WINDOWS

CRISP COLLAR

WEATHERED SKIN

PAMPHLET
ABOUT LOCAL
AREA

BACKPACK CONTAINS:
· WATER BOTTLE
· MUESLI BAR
· CHEESE AND
   BRANSTON PICKLE
   SANDWICHES

UNLIKE NORMAL
HUMANS, FRANK
DOESN'T SEEM
TO SWEAT

TUCKED IN

CASIO F-91W
(BEEPS ON
THE HOUR)

WOOLLY SOCKS

BUILT FOR
ENDURANCE

HI-TEC
BOOTS

HOSPO
VET
KENT

It's 8.30 p.m., and Kent's been at work since the breakfast shift started, just before 7 a.m. He would've gone home hours ago, but Tracy and Gavin called in sick, and he's not sure if he trusts Andrew to work the bar unsupervised. The dinner service is in full swing, and there's a rowdy school reunion in the main conference room, so Kent's sticking around to make sure none of the less experienced staff get in any trouble.

When he finally finishes work for the day (and night), he'll probably head home, strip down to his undies and zone out on the couch with a nice bottle of chardonnay. That's if Kent can leave quietly. Most likely, Rodney (the chef) will ask if he wants to stop at the casino on the way home for a cheeky beer and a gamble. Damn you, Rodney!

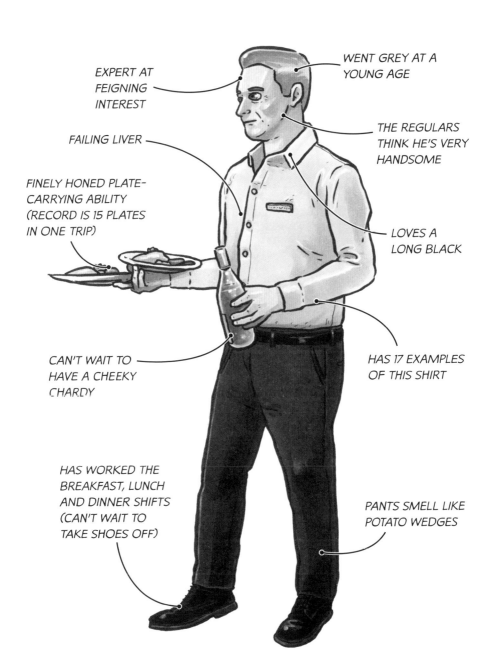

EXPERT AT FEIGNING INTEREST

WENT GREY AT A YOUNG AGE

FAILING LIVER

THE REGULARS THINK HE'S VERY HANDSOME

FINELY HONED PLATE-CARRYING ABILITY (RECORD IS 15 PLATES IN ONE TRIP)

LOVES A LONG BLACK

CAN'T WAIT TO HAVE A CHEEKY CHARDY

HAS 17 EXAMPLES OF THIS SHIRT

HAS WORKED THE BREAKFAST, LUNCH AND DINNER SHIFTS (CAN'T WAIT TO TAKE SHOES OFF)

PANTS SMELL LIKE POTATO WEDGES

PUBLICAN PAT

Dozens of staff have been and gone in the 15 years that Pat's been working at O'Reilly's, and to the regulars she's almost like part of the furniture. Who knows what the old boys would do if she weren't there to pour their drinks and lend an ear?

Pat's heard it all before, but you wouldn't think so when listening to her talk to the punters. She greets each new face like an old friend, laughs at every terrible joke she's told and smiles when the old fellas attempt to flirt with her. Pat tried to leave once; she managed to last about two weeks at an office job before she was back behind the bar.

O'Reilly's wouldn't be the same without you, Pat.

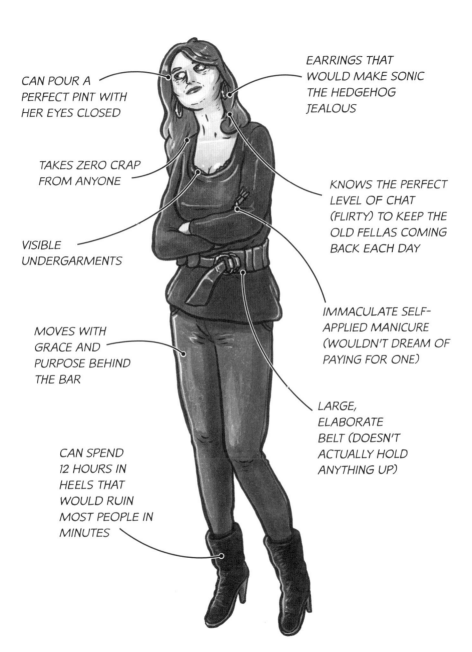

CAN POUR A PERFECT PINT WITH HER EYES CLOSED

EARRINGS THAT WOULD MAKE SONIC THE HEDGEHOG JEALOUS

TAKES ZERO CRAP FROM ANYONE

KNOWS THE PERFECT LEVEL OF CHAT (FLIRTY) TO KEEP THE OLD FELLAS COMING BACK EACH DAY

VISIBLE UNDERGARMENTS

MOVES WITH GRACE AND PURPOSE BEHIND THE BAR

IMMACULATE SELF-APPLIED MANICURE (WOULDN'T DREAM OF PAYING FOR ONE)

LARGE, ELABORATE BELT (DOESN'T ACTUALLY HOLD ANYTHING UP)

CAN SPEND 12 HOURS IN HEELS THAT WOULD RUIN MOST PEOPLE IN MINUTES

DAIRY FARMER KEV

Kev would love to say that he's enjoying himself right now, but being ankle-deep in cow turds is never a fun way to start the day. Sometimes he thinks about selling up and buying one of those fancy apartments on the waterfront in Tauranga, but what would he do? Kev's never been the type to sunbathe or potter about, and he's not sure he trusts anyone else with the family land.

He may be having a tough morning, but watching that sun rise over the valley gets him every time. He must've seen it about eight thousand times, each one different, each one just as stunning as the last. Dairy farming's not for everyone, but it's perfect for Kev. Good on ya, mate.

PERMANENT STUBBLE

PROUDLY WEARS THE COLOURS OF LOCAL SPORTS TEAM

THREE-COLLAR SET-UP:
1. SHIRT
2. JERSEY
3. JACKET

TIRED A. F.

SEEMINGLY ANCIENT, WEATHERED OILSKIN JACKET

FADED 20-YEAR-OLD RUGBY TOP

LEATHERY SKIN

CAN'T REMEMBER THE LAST TIME HE WASHED HIS JEANS

FUELLED BY HAM SANDWICHES WITH HOT ENGLISH MUSTARD

PROFESSIONAL-QUALITY GUMBOOTS (COVERED IN SHIT)

UIH

WORKOUT MISBAH

It's hard to ignore Misbah as he rolls up to the gym after work. The sound system in his Beemer rattles the gym windows and its dinner-table-sized chrome wheels gleam in the late sun like a meteoroid burning up in Earth's atmosphere.

Upon entry, Misbah is greeted by his workout crew, and after performing the usual bro hugs, they begin concocting their various protein shakes, pre-workout drinks, post-pre-workout gels, and pre-post-workout smoothies.

The crew's workout sessions are casual and quite lengthy, usually involving a few quick reps on a machine, followed by a social media cool-down and then some half-hearted poses in the mirror.

Much to the chagrin of the other gym-goers, Misbah's been getting great results from his indifferent workouts. What's his secret?

FANTASTIC HAIRLINE (BY FAR THE BEST IN THE GYM)

EARRING

THICK FACIAL HAIR GROWS SUPER QUICKLY (SHAVED THIS MORNING)

SPENDS 50% OF HIS GYM TIME ON THE PHONE

HIGH-QUALITY BLUETOOTH HEADPHONES (MAINLY WORN AS A NECKLACE)

G-SHOCK GA700-4A-RED (MATCHES TRACKIES)

SOLID GAINS (ONLY NEEDS TO LOOK AT WEIGHTS FOR MUSCLE TO APPEAR)

KEYS TO 2008 BMW M3 (LOWERED AND WITH GIANT WHEELS)

BLACK CANVAS SLIP-ONS

FITTED TRACKIES

COUNTRY JULIE

You couldn't dislike Julie if you tried: she's just so bloody nice! Julie's sons, Jackson and Damon, are currently competing in an inter-school rowing regatta and, true to form, Julie is there, helping out in any way she can. She's operating the school's snack trailer to make sure everyone's fuelled and hydrated. She loves being involved, and it's a great way to get to know the teachers, students and other parents.

It's becoming a tradition for the crew and their parents to come back to Julie's house for a post-event barbecue, and today is no different. She's already phoned ahead to her husband Tony and told him to fire up the burners and make sure the pool is clean. Nice one, Julie, you're a legend!

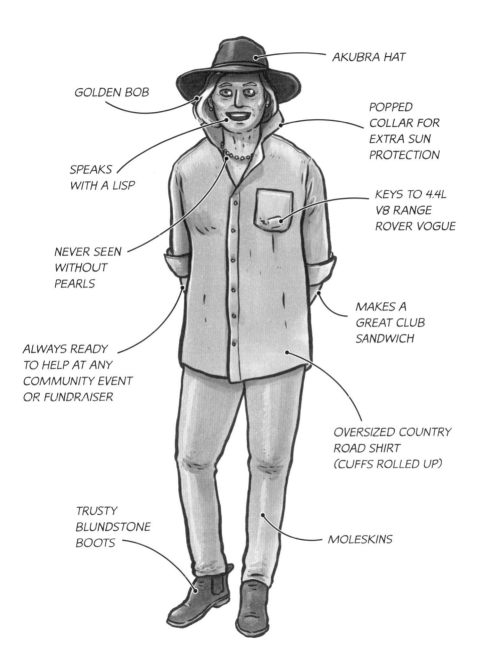

AKUBRA HAT

GOLDEN BOB

POPPED COLLAR FOR EXTRA SUN PROTECTION

SPEAKS WITH A LISP

KEYS TO 4.4L V8 RANGE ROVER VOGUE

NEVER SEEN WITHOUT PEARLS

MAKES A GREAT CLUB SANDWICH

ALWAYS READY TO HELP AT ANY COMMUNITY EVENT OR FUNDRAISER

OVERSIZED COUNTRY ROAD SHIRT (CUFFS ROLLED UP)

TRUSTY BLUNDSTONE BOOTS

MOLESKINS

CHEF RODNEY

As usual, the kitchen at the Red Lion Hotel is a swirling mess of sweaty bodies and delicious, heart-disease-stoking food. Rodney's lost count of the number of steak specials he's cooked tonight, and can't wait for a break in service to go out back for a cigarette.

Rodney can make anything on the Red Lion menu with his eyes closed and his hands tied behind his back; if you can stick it in your gob and eat it, Rodney's probably cooked it. To keep himself from becoming stale, Rodney's been developing some experimental dishes for a friend's food truck. On the menu this week are Korean BBQ chicken waffles, featuring his famous mayonnaise and apocalypse chillis.

Sounds bloody good, Rodney!

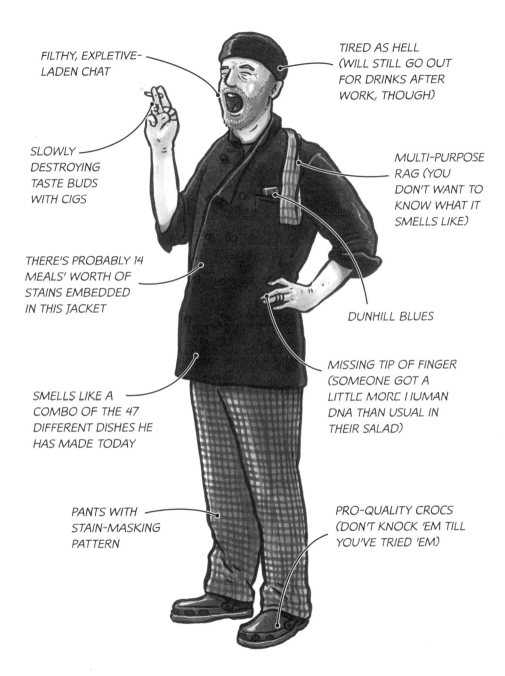

FILTHY, EXPLETIVE-LADEN CHAT

TIRED AS HELL (WILL STILL GO OUT FOR DRINKS AFTER WORK, THOUGH)

SLOWLY DESTROYING TASTE BUDS WITH CIGS

MULTI-PURPOSE RAG (YOU DON'T WANT TO KNOW WHAT IT SMELLS LIKE)

THERE'S PROBABLY 14 MEALS' WORTH OF STAINS EMBEDDED IN THIS JACKET

DUNHILL BLUES

SMELLS LIKE A COMBO OF THE 47 DIFFERENT DISHES HE HAS MADE TODAY

MISSING TIP OF FINGER (SOMEONE GOT A LITTLE MORE HUMAN DNA THAN USUAL IN THEIR SALAD)

PANTS WITH STAIN-MASKING PATTERN

PRO-QUALITY CROCS (DON'T KNOCK 'EM TILL YOU'VE TRIED 'EM)

MUSO KEITH

It's 1 p.m. and Keith's day is just getting started. He had two gigs last night, so he didn't end up getting home until the early hours of the morning.

Keith's one of the most experienced bass players around, and at last count he was a member of five different bands, ranging from Irish folk to classic rock. Keith's full of stories: buy him a few whiskies and he'll show you the lighter he supposedly got off Pete Townshend; buy him the whole bottle and he'll regale you with tales from the time he filled in for Ross Valory during Journey's '81 tour.

The heady days of the eighties are a lifetime ago, though, and although he still loves to perform, he prefers the quiet life.

When he's finished his breakfast cigarette he'll head over to the rest home to have a cup of tea with his mother. He knows he wasn't the best kid growing up and that she worried about him a lot, so he's trying to make it up to her while he still can.

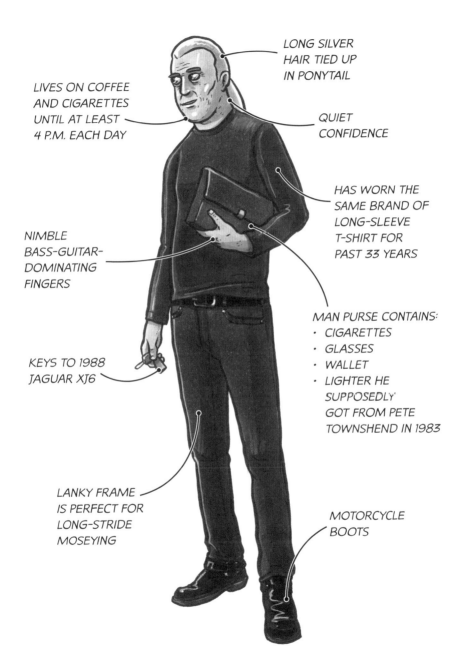

LONG SILVER HAIR TIED UP IN PONYTAIL

LIVES ON COFFEE AND CIGARETTES UNTIL AT LEAST 4 P.M. EACH DAY

QUIET CONFIDENCE

HAS WORN THE SAME BRAND OF LONG-SLEEVE T-SHIRT FOR PAST 33 YEARS

NIMBLE BASS-GUITAR-DOMINATING FINGERS

MAN PURSE CONTAINS:
· CIGARETTES
· GLASSES
· WALLET
· LIGHTER HE SUPPOSEDLY GOT FROM PETE TOWNSHEND IN 1983

KEYS TO 1988 JAGUAR XJ6

LANKY FRAME IS PERFECT FOR LONG-STRIDE MOSEYING

MOTORCYCLE BOOTS

CREATIVE MILO

Milo has always been creative; his mum says that he was drawing well before he could crawl and that his first word was *chiaroscuro* (that may be an exaggeration).

Milo is an integral part of the web department at Stiltonburger & Dangus, one of Auckland's leading creative agencies. The rest of the team would be lost without his sleek, user-friendly designs, and management loves his ability to upsell clients into paying for parallax scrolling sites.

When he's not creating cutting-edge websites, Milo enjoys browsing the GIF and cat sections of Reddit, adding to his extensive shoe collection and drinking artisanal coffee.

BLACK-FRAMED GLASSES

BEANIE WORN PURELY FOR LOOKS (NOT WARMTH)

ALWAYS SUPER POSITIVE

SHIRT BUTTONED UP TO TOP (NOT VERY COMFORTABLE)

WOULD HAVE A COCAINE HABIT IF COFFEE DIDN'T EXIST

$8000 EMAIL MACHINE (PERSONALISED)

CHUBBY MID-SECTION

STRUGGLES TO GET PHONE OUT OF PANTS

GLEAMING DOC MARTENS (HIS CURRENT PRIDE AND JOY)

STATEMENT PANTS

GIRLS' NIGHT ADELA

Things are getting pretty rowdy round at Adela's inner-city apartment: she's just cracked open her fourth Vodka Cruiser, the tunes are pumping loud, and the girls are all singing along (very badly).

If you think things seem messy in the living room, you don't want to see the rest of the house. You wouldn't believe the mess four young women can make getting ready for a night on the town.

The bathroom's littered with five sets of hair straighteners, 23 different shades of lipstick, 11 different toners, 10 sets of fake eyelashes, three discarded dresses, various empty bottles of bubbles, a broken stiletto and a box of Band-Aids.

Tayla's just ordered the Uber, so hopefully there's enough time to take a few selfies. What am I saying? Of course there's enough time for selfies!

HAIR CONTAINS AN
ENORMOUS AMOUNT
OF HAIRSPRAY

TOXIC-WASTE-
COLOURED
VODKA CRUISER

EARRINGS
MATCH EYES
AND NAILS

LOVES TO
SHOW OFF
'THE GIRLS'

EXTREMELY HIGH
SASS LEVELS

KEYS TO SUZUKI
SWIFT WITH
LEOPARD-PRINT
SEAT COVERS

LOVES ANIMAL-
THEMED SNAPCHAT
FILTERS

CAN'T BEND
LEGS IN
TIGHT JEANS

RIDICULOUSLY
LONG LEGS ARE
ALWAYS READY
TO BOOGIE

COMPLEX,
STRAPPY
FOOTWEAR

MORNING
BINS
MITCH

Mitch's Sunday morning isn't going well. Firstly, it's actually Monday morning, and secondly, it's bin day. Poor Mitch was peacefully dreaming of his future breakfast of bacon and eggs when off in the distance he heard the repetitive acceleration and braking of a rubbish truck.

Torn from his beautiful dream by the sound of his wife asking 'Did you take the bins out?', Mitch fell out of bed, grabbed the nearest dressing gown and commandeered his wife's slippers. Mitch has done bloody well to get the recycling bin out to the road before the truck arrives; too bad it's general rubbish day today. Recycling is next week.

BED HAIR

THOUGHT IT WAS SUNDAY MORNING

CRUST

HOPING THIS IS JUST AN EXTREMELY BORING DREAM

RECYCLING BIN (DON'T TELL HIM THAT IT'S RED BIN WEEK)

CORD IS THE ONLY THING BETWEEN HIM AND AN INDECENT EXPOSURE CHARGE

COULDN'T FIND MATCHING CORD (EYES WEREN'T WORKING YET)

TV REMOTE FROM LAST NIGHT

COLD BREEZE IS REFRESHING ON GENITALS

WIFE'S SLIPPERS (ACTUALLY KIND OF LIKES THEM)

SUPPLY
RUN
JEREMY

Jeremy (or Sasuke-Chan-SuperJ online) is more than a little sweaty after his walk home from the supermarket; he would've preferred to have done his supply run in the car, but his mum refused to drive him. It's Friday night and Jeremy is now fully stocked with everything he needs for a weekend of gaming. Jeremy's got a few hours before he meets up (online) with the rest of $lifer-Dragon-X (his clan), so he'll probably spend that time trolling a few forums and fuelling up on caffeinated beverages.

He knows he needs to start treating his body a little better, so he's looking at this weekend as one last binge session. Good luck, Sasuke-Chan-SuperJ!

EVERYONE ELSE IS STUPID

EXTENSIVE ANIME KNOWLEDGE

AUDIBLE BREATHING

ALWAYS TALKS ABOUT HIS ANNOYING FLATMATES (HIS PARENTS)

POP-CULTURE-THEMED T-SHIRT

ARMS HANG DOWN LIMPLY

LARGE BUT WEAK FRAME

BAG CONTAINS:
· TWO KINDS OF CHIPS
· SODA
· PIZZA SHAPES
· SIX-PACK OF CHOC MUFFINS

KNEES POINT IN

DEFORMED SLIP-ON SHOES

TOURIST GAËLLE

Gaëlle's had an amazing time travelling around New Zealand. Over the past few weeks, she's sunned herself on the golden beaches of the Coromandel, soaked in the steaming mineral springs of Rotorua and hiked the awe-inspiring tracks of the Abel Tasman National Park.

Gaëlle's just picked up a small campervan from Queenstown Airport, and can't wait to start the next leg of her adventure. Before she sets out on the long drive south to Fiordland National Park, Gaëlle's going to treat herself to a night in a hotel. She's no snob, but feels that a proper night's sleep without having to deal with a dorm full of snorers will do her the world of good. You should totally get room service, Gaëlle!

PRIMARY BANDANA

TRYING TO FIND SOMETHING TO DO (CAN'T WORK OUT WHY NOTHING SEEMS TO HAPPEN AFTER 8 P.M.)

GOLDEN LOCKS

FLAWLESS SKIN

SECONDARY BANDANA

GENERIC JACKET (ARE ALL EUROPEAN VISITORS ISSUED THESE?)

KEYS TO GARISHLY PAINTED TOYOTA PREVIA (FREEDOM CAMPER)

CASUAL SHOES

SENSIBLE WALKING SHOES

BOOT-CUT JEANS

TRAINER DANNIE

You may think that being a personal trainer is easy; let's face it, all Dannie seems to do is sit behind a desk and smile at people as they walk through the gym door. But the cheerful greeting is only part of the story. Can you imagine how tiring it is spending 45 minutes attempting to get a 65-year-old woman to do a crunch, knowing full well that she'll never turn up to her second PT session?

But that doesn't break Dannie's spirit. She lives in constant hope that her next client will actually listen to her advice by warming up correctly, squatting the full distance and maybe even eating right. Chin up, Dannie!

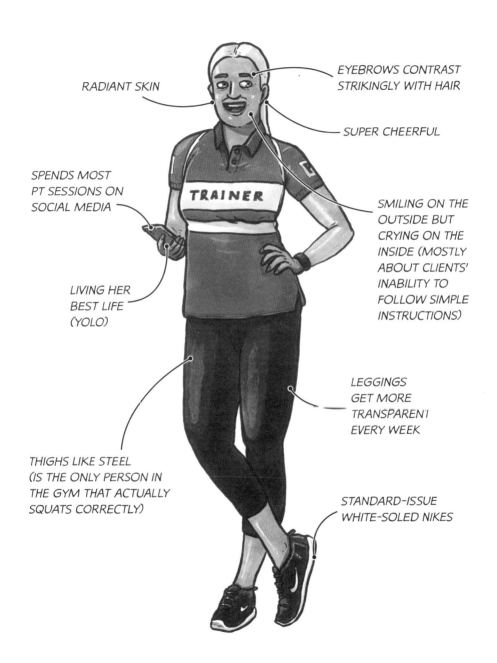

RADIANT SKIN

EYEBROWS CONTRAST STRIKINGLY WITH HAIR

SUPER CHEERFUL

SPENDS MOST PT SESSIONS ON SOCIAL MEDIA

TRAINER

SMILING ON THE OUTSIDE BUT CRYING ON THE INSIDE (MOSTLY ABOUT CLIENTS' INABILITY TO FOLLOW SIMPLE INSTRUCTIONS)

LIVING HER BEST LIFE (YOLO)

LEGGINGS GET MORE TRANSPARENT EVERY WEEK

THIGHS LIKE STEEL (IS THE ONLY PERSON IN THE GYM THAT ACTUALLY SQUATS CORRECTLY)

STANDARD-ISSUE WHITE-SOLED NIKES

CAREER POLITICIAN FRANCES

Frances became politically active after attending a Young Nationals meeting during university. It wasn't that the speaker was particularly good—in fact, it was the exact opposite. He was timid, dour and totally uninspiring; Frances knew she could do better, and that's exactly what she did. By her second year at uni, she was fully immersed in political life; there was no stopping her, and by year's end she was the Young Nats' president.

After finishing university, Frances spent nine years working in export sales, and although the pay was good and the work rewarding, she knew that politics was her calling.

She'd never stood for Parliament or any other office, but Frances decided to put her hat in the ring for the seat of her home electorate of East Coast Bays.

With the help of her far-reaching business connections and natural communication skills, Frances dominated the race. The rookie win shocked everyone but Frances: she'd always known she could do it.

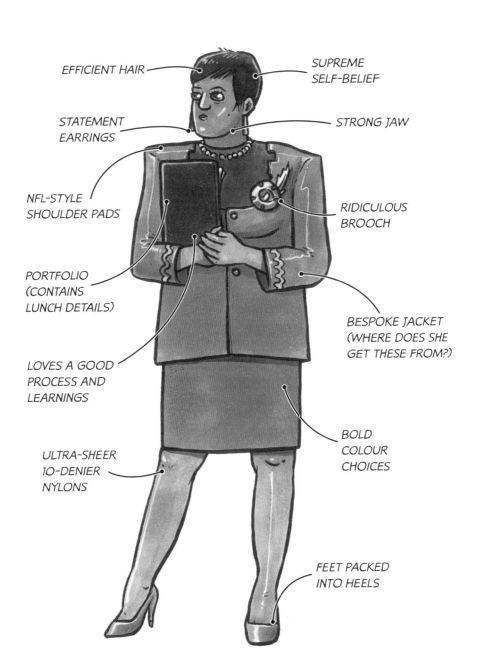

EFFICIENT HAIR

SUPREME SELF-BELIEF

STATEMENT EARRINGS

STRONG JAW

NFL-STYLE SHOULDER PADS

RIDICULOUS BROOCH

PORTFOLIO (CONTAINS LUNCH DETAILS)

BESPOKE JACKET (WHERE DOES SHE GET THESE FROM?)

LOVES A GOOD PROCESS AND LEARNINGS

ULTRA-SHEER 10-DENIER NYLONS

BOLD COLOUR CHOICES

FEET PACKED INTO HEELS

CAPTAIN KIWI

Things used to be simple for Captain Kiwi. He'd wake up at the crack of dawn, put on his woolly Swanndri top and tiny shorts, eat a meat pie for breakfast and wander into town to begin his day of superhero activities. Captain Kiwi was the guy you'd call if you needed things done. Having trouble changing your tyre? Captain Kiwi will sort it out. Need a tree stump removed from the garden? Captain Kiwi will bring the ute around to pull it out. Captain Kiwi was always there to help.

These days, life's a little more complicated for the Captain. His PR representative schedules all his activities through a smartphone app, and makes sure he documents every good deed on social media. This morning he's been told to pop into the office to go over some new merchandising concepts, then he's off to a $500-a-head luncheon with local city councillors, and he'll be finishing the day with a round of radio interviews to promote his new energy drink. Maybe the Captain needs a holiday.

TOWELLING HAT

CONFIDENT YET HUMBLE

HANDLEBAR MOUSTACHE

BALACLAVA

SWANNDRI JACKET

BEER

GARDENING GLOVES

RUGBY SOCKS

CLASSIC STUBBIES SHORTS

DOOR FROM 1985 TOYOTA HILUX (VIRTUALLY INDESTRUCTIBLE)

RUGBY BOOTS

SAM THE AUTHOR

Sam Moore's first drawing was a messy scribble of a train done with orange crayon on butcher's paper. His technique has improved in the 30-plus years since that creation, which is handy because he isn't very good at anything else.

Over the years, many companies have somehow let Sam work for them. He's designed countless prints for apparel, art-directed TV adverts and worked on numerous advertising campaigns.

When not creating colourful illustrations or coming up with creative ideas for clients, Sam enjoys eating food (especially Japanese and Korean), dog spotting, watching cricket (his body hurts too much to play it) and reading.

Sam lives in Christchurch, New Zealand with his wife Anna.

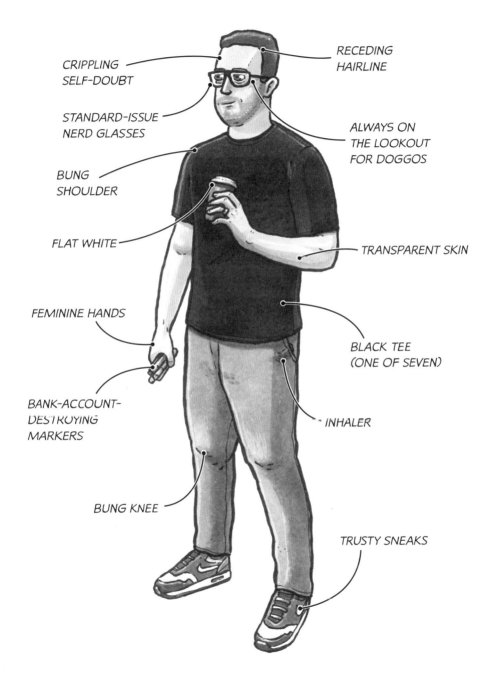

CRIPPLING
SELF-DOUBT

RECEDING
HAIRLINE

STANDARD-ISSUE
NERD GLASSES

ALWAYS ON
THE LOOKOUT
FOR DOGGOS

BUNG
SHOULDER

FLAT WHITE

TRANSPARENT SKIN

FEMININE HANDS

BLACK TEE
(ONE OF SEVEN)

INHALER

BANK-ACCOUNT-
DESTROYING
MARKERS

BUNG KNEE

TRUSTY SNEAKS

For Mum, Dad, Billie and Anna.
Without you, I would have lost my mind
long before this book was completed.

First published in 2019

Allen & Unwin
Level 3, 228 Queen Street
Auckland 1010, New Zealand
Phone: (64 9) 377 3800
Email: info@allenandunwin.com
Web: www.allenandunwin.co.nz

83 Alexander Street
Crows Nest NSW 2065, Australia
Phone: (61 2) 8425 0100

A catalogue record for this book is available from
the National Library of New Zealand.

ISBN 978 1 98854 712 1

Design by Kate Barraclough
Set in Gotham
Printed by C&C Offset Printing Co. Ltd, China

3 5 7 9 10 8 6 4 2